"In our modern vernacular [...] but good. It doesn't sound [...] ering in dismay in the sha [...] the Lord is the beginning [...] believers to understand wh [...] phrase. Christina leads us through Scripture to understand the phrase as God uses it. Christina is an able guide, and the reader will benefit from her thoughtful and thorough look at Scripture on fearing the Lord."

—Wendy Alsup is a mom, math teacher, and author of
Companions in Suffering: Comfort for Times of Loss and Loneliness

"We all struggle with fear and need to embrace the truths captured on these pages. Christina's clear and relatable words invite us to look past our fears and toward the Lord's love for us. She gently teaches us how to embark on a journey of growing in our reverence and awe of the Lord so we can find comfort in Him."

—Darby Strickland, CCEF counselor, teacher, and author of
*Is it Abuse? A Biblical Guide to Identifying Domestic
Abuse and Helping Victims*

"During a trial or challenging moment, we rarely take the time to analyze the fear underneath our anger, frustration, or anxiety. But if we were to place these lesser fears next to a greater fear of the Lord who has promised His presence, then that would be a trajectory changer. *A Holy Fear* provides that needed biblical perspective. Its pages are filled with a gospel primer to fight our lesser fears and replace them with a fear of the Lord that leads to walking in wisdom."

—Karen Hodge, coordinator of women's ministries for the
Presbyterian Church in America (PCA) and author of
Transformed: Life-taker to Life-giver and *Life-giving Leadership*

"Christina Fox invites readers to tread on holy ground agape with wonder for the utter perfection of God's nature. But the author doesn't stop there; she leads God-fearers from the glorious summit to practical daily life. Be aware: *A Holy Fear* will shrink your lesser fears, giving birth to profound adoration and worship of

the magnificent One who made us for His possession. Shoes are optional for this transformative pilgrimage led by a fellow traveler."
—Leslie Bennett, director of Women's Ministry Initiatives,
Revive Our Hearts

"Is it a surprising observation that we live in a fear-filled world? How does the Christian respond to cultures that seek to stoke those fears? Christina Fox shows us that the response to the world's fear is the right kind of fear: the fear of the Lord. This volume is an excellent aid in helping Christians unpack just what is the 'fear of the Lord' and how such a right fear can keep us from living fear-filled lives. I highly recommend it."
—Ike Reeder, president, Birmingham Theological Seminary

"This book couldn't have come at a better time. Every day we wake up to news reports and social media posts that fill our hearts with fear. Our neighbors are worried about finances, health, safety, and security. We are too. Thankfully, Christina Fox redirects our hearts in the pages of this book. Rather than fearing the daily worries of life in a fallen world, she tells us that we need to cultivate a holy fear of the eternal God who rules the universe. Only in rightly fearing God will we find rest from all our other fears. And in fearing God, we will find abundant life. With rich theology, careful Bible exposition, and helpful study questions, *A Holy Fear* will lead you by the hand to the place of safety and security we all desire."
—Megan Hill, author of *A Place to Belong: Learning to Love the Local Church*, editor for the Gospel Coalition, and pastor's wife

"As human beings we all have our fears and are all motivated by our fears. In their own way, our fears drive us and direct us. What Christina Fox does so well in this book is address the facts of our fears, diagnose the source of our fears, and prescribe the solution to our fears. As you read her book you will come to see that the cure to our fears is fear, for the problem at the heart of each human being is not *that* we fear, but *what* we fear. Or, better said, it's *who* we fear."
—Tim Challies, blogger, Challies.com

A Holy Fear

A Holy Fear

Trading Lesser Fears for the Fear of the Lord

Christina Fox

Reformation Heritage Books
Grand Rapids, Michigan

A Holy Fear
© 2020 by Christina Fox

Reformation Heritage Books
2965 Leonard St. NE
Grand Rapids, MI 49525
616–977–0889
orders@heritagebooks.org
www.heritagebooks.org

Printed in the United States of America
20 21 22 23 24 25/10 9 8 7 6 5 4 3 2 1

Library of Congress Cataloging-in-Publication Data

Names: Fox, Christina, author.
Title: A holy fear : trading lesser fears for the fear of the Lord / Christina Fox.
Description: Grand Rapids, Michigan : Reformation Heritage Books, [2020] | Includes bibliographical references.
Identifiers: LCCN 2020040314 (print) | LCCN 2020040315 (ebook) | ISBN 9781601788092 (paperback) | ISBN 9781601788108 (epub)
Subjects: LCSH: God (Christianity)—Worship and love. | Fear of God—Christianity.
Classification: LCC BV4817 .F695 2020 (print) | LCC BV4817 (ebook) | DDC 231/.042—dc23
LC record available at https://lccn.loc.gov/2020040314
LC ebook record available at https://lccn.loc.gov/2020040315

For additional Reformed literature, request a free book list from Reformation Heritage Books at the above regular or email address.

To my mother-in-law, Judy,

*who taught me the joy of fearing the Lord
in the face of lesser fears*

SAFE IN HIM, OUR TALL TOWER

The name of the LORD is a strong tower; the righteous run to it and are safe.

—Proverbs 18:10

When fear rolls in like a storm cloud
    and overshadows my mind,
I freeze and cower like a prey,
    My thoughts jumbled and confined.

I quit before I ever start;
    the journey is danger-filled—
all the unknowns, risks, and what if's.
    Life pauses at a standstill.

I live an observer of life,
    watching time pass on by me
while my fears consume and control.
    How I long to be set free!

Then I open Your Word and read
    of one good and full of grace.
The Great I AM who keeps and saves
    and calls me before His face.

He rules and reigns over all;
    None can thwart His will and plan.
All creation bows before Him—
    none can snatch me from His hand.

Before Him all fear fades and shrinks
at Yahweh's might and power.
When we fear Him above all else,
we're safe in Him, our tall tower.

—Christina Fox

CONTENTS

PREFACE

Dear Friend,

Have you ever had a conversation with someone that you never forgot? For the other person, it may not have been remarkable, but for you it was memorable—even life changing. In my life, one such conversation took place between my mother-in-law and me.

A number of years ago, our family went to a theme park together. I spent much of my time standing at the exit to each ride, waiting for my children to come out and tell me how amazing it was. At one point, my mother-in-law and I stood beneath a ride that was high in the air. I casually commented that since having children, I found myself having difficulty with heights. As I looked at the ride towering above me, I could already feel my stomach drop.

My mother-in-law commented, "I used to have a lot of fears. But since the worst thing imaginable happened and God brought me through it, I don't have much to fear anymore."

It was a brief interchange and probably one I would have forgotten but for the fact that I had so many fears in my life. I couldn't get her comment out of my mind, and it spurred me on to consider what it might look like to have less fear. It made me think about her widowhood at a young age and her testimony of God's grace in her life over the years since—of her faith and trust in who God is and what He has done. And I considered how a person progresses from having a great fear of things and circumstances to a great trust in our great God.

And that led me to study the fear of the Lord.

This book is about fear. It's an emotion we are all familiar with to one degree or another. While this book does touch on some of the fears we experience in this life, such as the fear of harm or of the future, the emphasis of the book is on a greater fear, the fear of the Lord. The Bible teaches us that to overcome our fear of lesser things, we must replace it with something greater. And what could be greater than God?

You might consider this book a systematic theology of sorts on the fear of the Lord. I will unpack what the Bible has to say about it. I will look at what it means to fear the Lord, why we are to fear the Lord, how to grow in that fear, the fruit of such fear in our lives, God's promises to those who fear Him, and what it looks like to trade our lesser fears for the fear of the Lord.

An additional note for those who experience fear: We are not just physical beings nor are we only spiritual beings; we are both, and as such, each aspect of our being affects the other. This means that our fears can affect us physically, or vice versa. Physical conditions that influence our moods, medication side effects, hormonal fluctuations, and lack of sleep can also affect our emotions. In addition, for people who have experienced trauma in their life, their bodies remember that trauma long after the fact, often causing them to feel haunted by their past. Whatever the reason, I encourage all who are gripped by fear to seek out proper medical care and wise Christian counseling.

No matter our circumstances, no matter what our lesser fears are, we all need to grow in the fear of the Lord. Join me on a journey as we dig into God's Word and learn what it means to fear Him.

Your fellow traveler,
Christina Fox

ACKNOWLEDGMENTS

I've had many prayer warriors lift up this project to the Lord on my behalf. I am grateful to Karen Hodge and the rest of the PCA Women's Ministry team for their encouragement and prayers. Thanks also to my small group at ECPC, who prays for me and my writing ministry. I am thankful to writing friends who pray for me and encourage me forward in my writing, including Holly Mackle, Megan Hill, and Sarah Ivill.

Thank you, Lisa Tarplee, for pointing me to my identity in Christ when I forget and need that reminder. I am thankful for your gospel friendship.

Thanks to Susan Hunt for her encouragement and guidance when I needed it most. Thanks also to my fellow coffee-loving friend, Maryanne Helms, for her prayers and encouragement.

Thank you to my mother-in-law, Judy, for her testimony of trust in the Lord. It has encouraged my heart and pointed me to the goodness of God.

I am grateful to my agent, Don Gates, and his labors on my behalf. Thank you to Reformation Heritage Books and Jay Collier, who believed in this project.

I am grateful to my readers and to the many women I have met while speaking at women's ministry events, conferences, and retreats. It is a joy to serve the church through writing and speaking. I not only have the opportunity to encourage others but I always receive it as well. I can relate to Paul's words in Romans 1:11–12: "For I long to see you, that I may impart to you some spiritual gift, so that you may be established—that is, that I may be encouraged together with you by the mutual faith both of you and me."

To my family—George, Ethan, and Ian—thank you for your continued support of my labors, your encouragement, and your prayers. I am grateful and love you.

Above all, I am thankful to the Lord for the opportunity to write on this topic, for it's one I have long been passionate about. I am grateful for the time to dig into God's Word and have my own heart pulled away from lesser fears to a greater and holy fear.

Chapter 1

A FEAR-FILLED LIFE

I remember it like it was yesterday. That tightness in my stomach and the way my heart seemed to beat loudly in my ears. The dryness in my mouth and the way my eyes started to fill with unshed tears. The way time seemed to freeze, and I had to ask the doctor to repeat what she just said because her voice seemed to come from far away.

I was at my annual physical checkup, and in response to my complaint about fatigue and difficulty regulating my body temperature, my doctor reached out to feel around the front of my neck. She said, "There's a lump here on your thyroid we need to get checked out. It could be cancerous." She then explained what it might mean and the next steps.

What followed were tests and visits to specialists followed by more tests. Complex statistics and facts swirled around my head. All the unknowns, the waiting, the pokes and prods kept me on edge for months. My mind was filled with thoughts of *What if*, *I can't*, and *Should I do this or that?* Eventually, I ended up having surgery to remove half my thyroid because of a precancerous growth. Needless to say, the entire experience was frightening to me.

Fear. It's a word we all are acquainted with. It can be a temporary emotion as well as a way of life. Our fears often keep us up at night and gnaw at us throughout the day, warning us of perceived dangers around every corner. They can stop us in our tracks and keep us from living our life. Our fears can govern our choices, shape the direction of our days, and rule over our hearts. And ultimately our fears can keep us from trusting in and resting in God.

A Fear-Filled World

It's hard to imagine, but there was a time when fear did not exist. There was a place where there wasn't anything to fear. In this place, there were no germs or illnesses or death. There were no enemies or violence. There was no such thing as failure, loss, or uncertain futures. If there were creepy-crawlies, they didn't creep anyone out. Because nothing bad happened, there was nothing of which to be afraid.

Where was this place? The *garden of Eden.*

When God created the world, He said it was good. Everything worked as it should. Our first parents, Adam and Eve, enjoyed perfect communion with God and with each other. They enjoyed their work as vice-regents over all God had made. They knew God and were known by Him—until the day they defied God's command not to eat from the Tree of Knowledge of Good and Evil. In doing so, sin then entered the world and with it the curse of death (see Rom. 5:12). Adam's immediate response to his sin was fear. When God called out for him and asked him where he was, he responded, "I heard Your voice in the garden, and I was afraid because I was naked; and I hid myself" (Gen. 3:10). From then on, this world became a fear-filled place, and we've all responded like our first parents: we've become fear-filled hiders, covering ourselves to remain out of God's sight.

Adam and Eve were cast out of the garden and away from the presence of God. The impact of sin in the world was instant. Adam and Eve's son Cain murdered his brother, Abel. The Bible tells us that by the time of Noah, the "wickedness of man was great in the earth, and…every intent of the thoughts of his heart was only evil continually" (Gen. 6:5). The Bible recounts story after story of the impact of the fall on people's hearts and on the created world.

The fall explains why fear exists. Because of the fall, the potential for harm, chaos, loss, and even death haunts us each day. It's a constant shadow that follows us wherever we go. And in a fallen world, there are plenty of reasons to feel fear: terrorism, assault, pandemics, incurable diseases, modern-day slavery, tornadoes, stock exchange plummets, and more. To make matters worse, we can learn about such fearful things on a 24/7 news cycle.

> *Our fears can govern our choices, shape the direction of our days, and rule over our hearts.*

Before we go further, I do want to point out that fear is a helpful and important emotion when we come face-to-face with genuine danger, for it gets us to respond and flee from harm. It's what gets us out of the building when there's a fire or to head to the basement when the tornado sirens sound. The Puritan John Flavel referred to this as "natural fear": "Everyone experiences natural fear. It is the trouble or agitation of mind that arises when we perceive approaching evil or impending danger. It is not always sinful, but it is always the fruit and consequence of sin."[1] Flavel then points out that our Savior, in taking on human flesh, experienced natural fear. One such example took place the night before He was betrayed: "Jesus came with them to a place called Gethsemane, and said to the disciples, 'Sit here while I go and pray over there.' And He took with Him Peter and the two sons of Zebedee, and He began to be sorrowful and deeply distressed. Then He said to them, 'My soul is exceedingly sorrowful, even to death. Stay here and watch with Me'" (Matt. 26:36–38). Take a moment to pause and think about what it means that Jesus lived in a fear-filled world. He knew the natural fear we all know so well. In the garden of Gethsemane, He sweat drops of blood as He thought about the horrors to come at the cross. Yet "for the joy that was set before Him [He] endured the cross, despising the shame, and has sat down at the right hand of the throne of God" (Heb. 12:2). What amazing grace!

The fear we will focus on in this chapter is not natural fear, but the fear that grips and rules our hearts. It's the kind that becomes a pattern in our lives, an immediate response to our circumstances. It's the kind of fear that distracts us and keeps us from resting and trusting in God and His great love for us.

We will consider fears such as these:

---

1. John Flavel, *Triumphing Over Sinful Fear* (Grand Rapids: Reformation Heritage Books, 2011), 8.

- Your spouse comes home from work and shares a rumor going around the office that pink slips loom on the horizon. You begin to worry and fear about what will happen if jobs are cut. How will you pay the bills? Will you lose your home? What will you do?

- You are invited to participate in a dream project for work. It's something you've always wanted to do, yet you start thinking about how ill-prepared you are for it. It's bigger than anything you've ever tackled before. You don't know what you are doing. What if you fail? You hesitate to accept the invitation and begin listing reasons why you can't participate.

- Your child wants to go away to summer camp with his buddies. You've heard great things about the camp and know many children who have attended. Yet you hesitate. What if he gets sick while away from home? What if he gets injured? What if something terrible happens?

- Your annual blood work came back with some concerns, and your doctor leaves a message asking you to return for more tests. You immediately imagine the worst. You think of all the horrible things that could happen. You think of your children being left without a parent. Before you know it, your fears have a choke hold on you, and you can barely breathe.

Sometimes, as in the case of my cancer scare, our fears can start out as natural fear and develop into sinful fear. For example, when my older son was little, he was sick all the time. He had chronic infections that exacerbated his asthma. I spent many a late night giving him breathing treatments, wondering if he would ever get better. It seemed like we were at the doctor's office nearly every week for months.

We were sent from one medical expert to the next, and by the time he was four, the doctor said my son needed to have sinus surgery. At that time, such surgeries were rarely done on young children because of the risks involved. To be honest, I was terrified. So many things could have gone wrong. I sat in the hospital waiting room filled with fear and thinking through all the worst-case scenarios.

Then a friend called me, and I sat out in the hallway, voicing my fears to her with tears running down my face. She prayed with me over the phone, both for my heart and for the outcome of my son's surgery.

You are likely familiar with such fears. We all feel some degree of worry when a loved one faces a frightening diagnosis or surgery. We may fear the pain they will experience. We might fear losing them to their illness. But that's not the only thing we fear. Some of us might fear specific things, such as flying on an airplane or speaking in public. We also can fear being left out or being rejected by others. We can fear losing something dear to us, whether a relationship, a job, or a dream. We can fear failure. We can even fear the unknown future.

When we take a close-up look at our fears, we see that they are closely related to what we desire, cherish, and value. They are associated with our loves and longings. We often fear losing what we hold dear. We find ourselves clinging tighter to what we have out of fear it will be ripped from us. Our fears also seem to taunt us, reminding us that we are vulnerable and weak. They reveal our neediness and point out that we don't have control over our lives. As Ed Welch writes, "Any time you love or want something deeply, you will notice fear and anxieties because you might not get them. Any time you can't control the fate of those things you want or love, you will notice fears and anxieties because you might lose them."[2]

Some fears seem to come and go. The frightening circumstance passes and with it our fears. But for some of us, there are times when we can't stop thinking about the things that we fear. We find ourselves fearful even when there is no reason to be. Then we start to feel our fear physically. Our body tells us something is wrong as our heart rate increases, our head hurts, and we feel nauseous. Our palms sweat and our breath quickens. Our worries and fears start to interfere with our sleep and eating habits. We have difficulty concentrating or sitting still. Over time, our work and home life begin to suffer. This is called anxiety, and it is a growing problem in our culture. About 18 percent of Americans are treated for anxiety,[3] making it the most common mental health issue today.

---

2. Ed Welch, *Running Scared: Fear, Worry, and the God of Rest* (Greensboro, N.C.: New Growth Press, 2007), 28.

3. Jamie Ducharme, "A Lot of Americans Are More Anxious than They Were Last Year, a New Poll Says," *Time*, May 8, 2018, http://www.time.com/5269371/americans-anxiety-poll/.

> *When we take a*
> *close-up look at*
> *our fears,*
> *we see that they*
> *are closely related*
> *to what we*
> *desire, cherish,*
> *and value.*

Responses to Fear

In the face of fear, we often feel helpless. I don't know about you, but I hate that feeling. As a result, I tend to try to find a solution to my fears, a way to regain some control over them. I study and research all that I fear, thinking that the more I know perhaps the more I can manage and contain it. I then plot and plan and develop solutions to my fears. I put my hope and trust in those solutions; I turn to them to make my life comfortable, better, and safer.

Because of my son's chronic illnesses as a young child, I was always fearful and on guard regarding his health. I worried about him catching illnesses from other children. I feared the long-term consequences of all the medication he had to take. I feared what might happen if we couldn't manage his asthma. I found myself doing everything I could to keep him healthy. I googled and searched for solutions. I had our home inspected for mold and removed all the carpets. I faithfully used hand sanitizer and kept my son away from other sick children.

Ultimately, those solutions became my idol, what I worshiped instead of God. I placed my trust and hope in them. That's the problem with our fears. While fear is a normal emotional response to life in a fallen world, when it grips our heart, we turn our gaze away from God and to the circumstances around us. We focus on the problem instead of the One who rules over all things. We place our trust not in God to help and rescue us but in things, methods, or even ourselves. This is idolatry.

But that's not the only way we respond to fear. Sometimes fear immobilizes us. We stand before it frozen, like a deer caught in a car's headlights. Perhaps we face a big decision in life, and because we fear making the wrong decision, we don't make one at all. Life moves on around us, and we simply stay where we are. Or we zero in on the details of something and don't move forward until we get it perfect. We go over it and over it because we want to get it right the first time. Years go by, and we haven't moved forward because we're still waiting for that all-too-elusive perfection.

Throughout childhood I played the flute. I wasn't the best at it, but I enjoyed doing it. I played in the school band and for my church. When I went to college, the music department offered individual classes for those who played musical instruments. Oh, how I wanted to take one of those classes! But fear held me back. I feared that I wasn't good enough. I feared what the teacher would think of me. I feared wasting money on something at which I could never excel. Today, I look back on that decision with regret.

Sometimes our fears don't keep us still but instead make us run away. The first sign of something harmful, and we split. We'd rather escape and live on a deserted island, far away from any danger, than to face head on what we fear. In the state of our current culture, it's hard not to respond this way. Consider all the frightening things our children face when they walk out the front door each morning: bullying and school violence, online predators, school systems that want to shape their minds, and a post-truth culture seeking to influence them at every turn. It's hard not to fear such a world. It's hard not to want to run and hide. Yet such fear makes the world bigger and stronger than the God who holds the world in the palm of His hands.

Responses like these eventually fail us. Whether we try to control our fears, freeze, or run away from them, they still linger, mocking us. They still rule over us. They still keep us looking at what we fear rather than trusting the Lord. Hang in with me though; there's hope ahead for the fear-filled heart.

Let's look at what the Bible has to say about fear. As it turns out, it has a lot to say.

Do Not Fear

While I haven't personally counted all the instances, commands in Scripture not to fear are generally considered the most common. In both the Old and New Testaments, the command "Do not fear" is given in numerous situations and circumstances. Whether facing real terror and pending harm or worries about tomorrow's provision, God's people are called not to fear. This command is often found in the context of divine revelation, such as when God's people were called to fight a battle or when a prophet warned of pending punishment for sin. Such a command is intended to comfort God's people and to encourage them to trust in Him, as in the following examples from the Old Testament:

> Moses said to the people, "Do not be afraid. Stand still, and see the salvation of the LORD, which He will accomplish for you today. For the Egyptians whom you see today, you shall see again no more forever." (Ex. 14:13)

Fear not, for I am with you;
Be not dismayed, for I am your God.
I will strengthen you,
Yes, I will help you,
I will uphold you with My righteous right hand.
(Isa. 41:10)

Before we go further, we should pause and consider the meaning behind such a command. That's because words are important. We use words every day, often without thinking of their significance. In the English language, words often have multiple meanings and nuances, depending on the context. As we begin to look at the fear of the Lord, it is helpful to look at how the Bible uses words like *fear*, *worry*, or *anxiety*.

The most common Hebrew word for fear found in the Bible is *yirah*.[4] It is used to mean "terror," like when the Bible describes how the men on the ship with Jonah responded when they were caught in a deadly storm: "Then the men were exceedingly afraid, and said to him, 'Why have you done this?'" (Jonah 1:10). It is also used to mean "reverence," specifically in the context of the fear of the Lord: "The fear of the LORD is the beginning of wisdom" (Ps. 111:10).

In the New Testament, the Greek word used for fear is *phobos*.[5] It means "panic," "flight," or "terror." It's where we get the English word *phobia*. For example, when the disciples saw Jesus walking on the water, they responded with fear: "When the disciples saw Him walking on the sea, they were troubled, saying, 'It is a ghost!' And they cried out for fear"

---

4. *Strong's Concordance*, s.v. "*yirah*," https://biblehub.com/hebrew/3374.htm.
5. *Strong's Concordance*, s.v. "*phobos*," https://biblehub.com/greek/5401.htm.

(Matt. 14:26). It's also used to mean "awe and reverence," as in Luke's description of the early church: "Then fear came upon every soul, and many wonders and signs were done through the apostles" (Acts 2:43).

> Whether we try to control our fears, freeze, or run away from them, they still linger, mocking us.

Context clearly matters when it comes to the word *fear*. When the Bible tells us not to fear something, it is referring to terror or panic. When it talks about the fear of the Lord, it means having awe or reverence, which we'll explore in the next chapter.

Because excessive worry and anxiety are such close cousins to fear, it's interesting to look at the Greek word for anxiety, *merimnaó*. It is used in Jesus's Sermon on the Mount when He says not to worry or be anxious about tomorrow (Matt. 6:25–34) and also in Philippians 4:6, when Paul cautions us not to be anxious about anything. *Merimnaó* means "to be anxious, to care for." Its Greek root word means "to be divided, to be pulled apart."[6] This is what happens to us when we are consumed with worry about something. Our minds are distracted from everything else but our worries. These thoughts pull at and divide us. As Flavel wrote, "The sinfulness of fear consists in the distracting influence it has upon the heart, whereby it unfits us for the discharge of our duties."[7] Instead, God wants us to look away from our

---

6. *Strong's Concordance*, s.v. "*merimnaó*," https://biblehub.com/greek/3309.htm.

7. Flavel, *Triumphing Over Sinful Fear*, 17.

troubles and to Him alone—to place our trust in Him to meet our needs.

While we can fear just about anything, the Bible mentions a few specific fears: the fear of man, the fear of harm, and the fear of the future.

Fear of Man

The fear of man is a common fear for all of us. This can refer to fearing harm at the hand of someone else. The Bible is filled with accounts of God's people fearing other nations that were seemingly bigger and stronger than they. When the spies were sent into the land of Canaan to assess what was there, all but two of the spies returned with a fearful report about giants in the land (Numbers 13).

The fear of man also refers to the fear of what people think of us. We might fear what they say about us to others. We might fear their rejection. When we fear man, we want the approval and praise of others and will conform and change our behavior in order to receive it. When Peter refused to eat with the Gentiles, he feared what the Judaizers thought of him (Gal. 2:11–13). Ed Welch says that the fear of man sees "people as 'bigger' (that is, more powerful and significant) than God, and, out of the fear that creates in us, we give other people the power and right to tell us what to feel, think, and do."[8]

The fear of man then becomes an idol that we worship. We seek the affirmation and acceptance of others, looking to that

---

8. Ed Welch, *When People Are Big and God Is Small* (Greensboro, N.C.: New Growth Press, 2011), 23.

affirmation to give our lives value and meaning. But because we look to broken and fallen people to meet our needs, this idol will inevitably fail us and let us down. No wonder the book of Proverbs cautions, "The fear of man brings a snare, but whoever trusts in the LORD shall be safe" (29:25).

Fear of Harm

Because we live in a fallen world where danger exists, the Bible also speaks of the fear of harm. When the disciples were sailing on the Sea of Galilee with Jesus, a great storm arose. Though some of them were seasoned fishermen and were used to storms at sea, they were terrified. Jesus was asleep, and they went to wake Him up:

> "Lord, save us! We are perishing!"
> But He said to them, "Why are you fearful, O you of little faith?" Then He arose and rebuked the winds and the sea, and there was a great calm. (Matt. 8:25–26)

As we saw earlier, there is much to fear in a fallen world. Whether we fear a natural disaster, sickness and disease, or violent enemies, whenever the Bible speaks of the fear of harm, it then points to who God is and what He has done. It reminds us to turn and look to Him for help and rescue. When Jesus calmed the storm at sea, notice that it didn't gradually calm down, like when a storm system moves on to another location. Rather, this storm stopped in an instant. Just as when the first light at creation appeared at God's command, this storm stopped at the Creator's voice. The Bible tells us, "The men marveled, saying, 'Who can this be, that even the winds and the sea obey Him?'" (Matt. 8:27). In that moment, they saw that the Lord was greater than all their fears.

Fear of the Future

In a sense, all our fears are fears of the future. That's because fear likes to time travel, looking ahead to possible harms and warning us of all that could go wrong. Future fear is worried about whether there will be enough in the days to come: enough money, enough food, enough time, enough wisdom, enough strength. We fear future losses and failures. We fear not being prepared or knowing what to do in a situation. We fear the unknown.

As mentioned earlier, Jesus told us not to worry about not having enough because our heavenly Father provides for all our needs: "Therefore do not worry about tomorrow, for tomorrow will worry about its own things. Sufficient for the day is its own trouble" (Matt. 6:34). As John Calvin wrote, "Believers ought to rely on God's fatherly care, to expect that he will bestow upon them whatever they feel to be necessary, and not to torment themselves by unnecessary anxiety."[9]

The Bible doesn't teach that we are to not have any cares or worries at all. There is a certain amount of care we need to take in this life. We should have concerns about things. We should get up each morning and labor to feed our families. We should have concern about our children's health and take them to the doctor for treatment when they are ill. Even Paul described his concerns and cares for the churches he

---

9. John Calvin, *Commentary on Matthew*, https://biblehub.com/commentaries/calvin/matthew/6.htm.

> *The Bible doesn't teach that we are to not have any cares or worries at all.... It's when those cares become excessive, to the point that we don't trust God for tomorrow's needs, that our worries and fears become sinful.*

ministered to (2 Cor. 11:28). It's when those cares become excessive, to the point that we don't trust God for tomorrow's needs, that our worries and fears become sinful. Or that they cause us to rely solely on ourselves instead of crying out to God for help. Calvin commented, "He does not forbid every kind of care, but only what arises from distrust."[10]

What are we to do when we have any of these fears? What do we do when we hear rumors of job cuts or a loved one is seriously ill or the dream we've worked so hard for looks like it will fail? What do we do in the face of such fears? As we'll see next and unpack throughout this book, the Bible calls us to turn from our fears toward a greater fear.

A Greater Fear

Have you ever voiced your fears to someone and he or she responded with a seemingly trite answer, such as "You just need to trust God more"? Inside you think, "It's just not that easy." We can read the Bible's admonitions not to fear as trite responses as well. But we shouldn't. When God tells us not to fear, He's not saying that we need to just believe more. He's not saying we just need to have faith that everything will be

---

10. Calvin, *Commentary on Matthew.*

okay, and it will. Instead, He calls us to something greater—to *Someone* greater.

In addition to the command not to fear, another command in Scripture is also prevalent, and it also involves fear. But rather than a command not to fear something, this is a command to fear. It is a call to a greater fear, a holy fear—the *fear of the Lord*.

In Matthew 10, after Jesus had called all the disciples to follow Him, He prepared to send them out to preach that the kingdom of God was at hand. He told them to heal the sick, raise the dead, and cast out demons. He warned them that some people would listen to them and some would reject their teaching. He also warned them of future persecution, that they would be hated and beaten and brought to trial. It is amid these warnings that He also taught them about the fear of the Lord:

> Whatever I tell you in the dark, speak in the light; and what you hear in the ear, preach on the housetops. And do not fear those who kill the body but cannot kill the soul. But rather fear Him who is able to destroy both soul and body in hell. Are not two sparrows sold for a copper coin? And not one of them falls to the ground apart from your Father's will. But the very hairs of your head are all numbered. Do not fear therefore; you are of more value than many sparrows. (vv. 27–31)

This passage teaches us that a fear of the Lord quells and weakens our lesser fears. The disciples were to replace their fear of harm from man with a fear of the Lord. While man might harm them physically, even to the point of death, God has power over the destination of their souls. He is the sovereign One who knows the number of hairs on their head. He cares for them more than the creatures He watches over each day. God is the one whom they were to fear.

The Bible teaches us that when we are fearful, we are to replace that fear with a greater fear, the fear of the Lord. What does that mean? We might compare it to a person consumed with worry about a job promotion she has long worked hard to achieve. She hears rumors around the office that someone else is being considered for the promotion as well. She grows fearful, thinking, "What if I don't get the promotion? It's what I've worked so hard for. I'll be stuck in this same job forever." Then she gets a call from her best friend, who just found out her company has filed for bankruptcy and she's been laid off from her job. "At least I still have a job," she thinks to herself. In this scenario, she sees losing a job as a greater fear than losing her promotion. The loss of her promotion weakened in the face of not having a job altogether. In a similar way, when we see God as bigger and greater than what we fear, our other fears grow weak. For example, let's say we face some kind of job uncertainty. In fearing the Lord, we would remind our heart that God owns all things. All we have comes from His generous hand. He is Jehovah Jireh, our provider. He promises to meet all our needs. We would remember all the times He provided for us in the past. Above all, we would dwell on His generous provision of grace for us in Christ. The more we dwell on who God is and what He has done, our fears lose their grip on us, for we'll see God as greater.

Join me on a journey to trade our lesser fears with a holy fear, a fear of the Lord. The first step is to explore just what it means to fear the Lord. That comes next.

Chapter 2

FEAR THE LORD

One of the things my husband and I have always enjoyed is traveling together. We love to explore new places and see things we've only read about or viewed in pictures.

A few years ago, we took a family vacation to Yosemite National Park in northern California. Half Dome, an iconic rock formation in the park, is a mountain picture I've seen countless times in my life, but to see it in person was nothing less than extraordinary. The park itself is huge, over a thousand square miles.

We took our kids on a few hikes, enjoying the brisk spring mountain weather. We marveled at the giant trees covered in mosses of varying shades of green. On one such hike, we came to spots in the trail where there were deep crevasses. One misstep, and we would fall thousands of feet to our death. There were no signs warning us, and my heart skipped a beat each time we passed one.

We got to the end of the trail and saw a crowd up ahead of us, taking in the view. We waited in line for our turn at the railing so we could take a family picture. When we got there, I could see how far down the drop was to the forest floor below—and that railing must have been installed when the park first opened in 1890. It looked rickety and weak. I started to feel dizzy and sick to my stomach. My heart was pounding in my ears. I couldn't look. I took a huge step back away from the railing. I grabbed my son's hand to pull him with me.

The picture we took that day shows me with a pained grimace. It's an accurate photo because I was pained. I was afraid. I was so excited about hiking in Yosemite, yet when I got to see the view, I couldn't look for fear of falling.

When we consider what it means to fear the Lord, is that what we are talking about? Is it terror and dread? Is it that feeling I had standing at the railing—nauseous, pale, and short of breath? Is the fear of the Lord the same thing as being afraid—as being terrified of God and wanting to run the other way?

The fear of the Lord is not a simple thing to define. It's not like looking up the definition of *fear* in the dictionary and finding a word or phrase that fully explains it. There are layers to it. Like a diamond has a multifaceted surface, so does the fear of the Lord. It takes multiple words to describe the various aspects of fearing the Lord. In fact, it's easier to describe than to provide a simple definition. That's what we are going to explore in this chapter.

Fear the Lord
While the Bible says hundreds of times "Do not fear," it also commands us to fear the Lord. It's an important command, one that we find in both the Old and New Testaments.

Old Testament

The LORD commanded us to observe all these statutes, to fear the LORD our God, for our good always, that He might preserve us alive, as it is this day. (Deut. 6:24)

Fear the LORD, serve Him in sincerity and in truth, and put away the gods which your fathers served on the other side of the River and in Egypt. Serve the LORD! (Josh. 24:14)

Oh, fear the LORD, you His saints! There is no want to those who fear Him. (Ps. 34:9)

The fear of the LORD is the beginning of knowledge, but fools despise wisdom and instruction. (Prov. 1:7)

Let us hear the conclusion of the whole matter:
Fear God and keep His commandments, For this is man's all. (Eccl. 12:13)

New Testament

Do not fear those who kill the body but cannot kill the soul. But rather fear Him who is able to destroy both soul and body in hell. (Matt. 10:28)

Then the churches throughout all Judea, Galilee, and Samaria had peace and were edified. And walking in the fear of the

> *Let us hear the conclusion of the whole matter:*
>
> *Fear God and keep His commandments, For this is man's all. (Eccl. 12:13)*

Lord and in the comfort of the Holy Spirit, they were multiplied. (Acts 9:31)

He who is mighty has done great things for me,
And holy is His name.
And His mercy is on those who fear Him
From generation to generation. (Luke 1:49–50)

Having these promises, beloved, let us cleanse ourselves from all filthiness of the flesh and spirit, perfecting holiness in the fear of God. (2 Cor. 7:1)

Who shall not fear You, O Lord, and glorify Your name?
For You alone are holy.
For all nations shall come and worship before You,
For Your judgments have been manifested. (Rev. 15:4)

Some people might think that fearing the Lord is reserved for the Old Testament, but as we can see, it's commanded in the New Testament as well. It's a quality for us as Christians to live out in our lives. And it's a quality so important that the teacher in Ecclesiastes described it as the whole duty of man. Let's begin by looking at two different ways a person can fear the Lord.

Servile versus Filial Fear

Sinclair Ferguson describes two different kinds of fear in the Bible: *filial fear* and *servile fear*.[1] Servile fear is like the fear slaves have for their cruel master or that of prisoners for their jailer. Slaves or prisoners obey out of fear of harm because

---

1. Sinclair Ferguson, *Grow in Grace* (Edinburgh: Banner of Truth, 1989), 28–29.

they know the master or jailer could hurt them at the slightest infraction. The only motivation for obeying is fear of harm. With servile fear, slaves or prisoners obey only to the extent that such obedience will keep them out of trouble. It is this kind of fear the unregenerate have for God and the kind of fear we have before coming to know Christ. It is true terror of God.

A good example of this is in Matthew 25 in the parable of the servants who were given talents to invest by their master. One servant just buried his in the ground: "Then he who had received the one talent came and said, 'Lord, I knew you to be a hard man, reaping where you have not sown, and gathering where you have not scattered seed. And I was afraid, and went and hid your talent in the ground. Look, there you have what is yours'" (vv. 24–25).

Filial fear, on the other hand, is the fear children have for their father. The word *filial* comes from the Latin, meaning "son." Children who know they are loved by their father obey him because they don't want to disappoint him or let him down. It is a respectful fear, a fear that honors. It is not a fear of terror, but a fear born out of love.

Outside of Christ, we would have a servile fear of God. But in Christ, we are adopted as God's children. Paul writes about this in Galatians 4:4–7:

> But when the fullness of the time had come, God sent forth His Son, born of a woman, born under the law, to redeem those who were under the law, that we might receive the adoption as sons.
>
> And because you are sons, God has sent forth the Spirit of His Son into your hearts, crying out, "Abba,

Father!" Therefore you are no longer a slave but a son, and if a son, then an heir of God through Christ.

Through the gift of justification, we are made children of the Father. J. I. Packer wrote, "The adopted status of believers means that in and through Christ God loves them as he loves his only-begotten Son and will share with them all the glory that is Christ's."[2] God is our Father, and like our earthly father He loves us, provides for us, protects us, disciplines us, and teaches us. Because God is our Father, the fear we have for Him is a filial fear.

For people who did not have a good relationship with their earthly father—or had no relationship at all—it can be hard to understand a concept like fearing the Lord with filial fear. If our experience with our earthly father was filled with conflict, anger, or abuse, we might expect the same of God. We might respond to God as though He is out to get us. We might expect Him to fail us. We may have trouble trusting Him to provide for us and meet our needs. We may look at the challenges and trials in our life as punishment from an angry God rather than loving discipline and training from our good Father.

Hebrews 12:7–11 teaches us:

If you endure chastening, God deals with you as with sons; for what son is there whom a father does not chasten? But if you are without chastening, of which all have become partakers, then you are illegitimate and not sons. Furthermore, we have had human fathers

2. J. I. Packer, *Concise Theology: A Guide to Historic Christian Beliefs* (Carol Stream, Ill.: Tyndale, 1993), 167.

who corrected us, and we paid them respect. Shall we not much more readily be in subjection to the Father of spirits and live? For they indeed for a few days chastened us as seemed best to them, but He for our profit, that we may be partakers of His holiness. Now no chastening seems to be joyful for the present, but painful; nevertheless, afterward it yields the peaceable fruit of righteousness to those who have been trained by it.

We have to remember that God is a perfect Father; all He does is good. His love for us will never wane. He is not fickle; He will not change. What He promises He will fulfill. While our earthly father may have failed us, hurt us, and been untrustworthy, our God is a good Father. Even His discipline and training are perfect and just what we need to grow in holiness. We can fear Him with a filial fear.

> *While our earthly father may have failed us, hurt us, and been untrustworthy, our God is a good Father.… We can fear Him with a filial fear.*

Sinclair Ferguson defines *filial fear* as "that indefinable mixture of reverence and pleasure, joy and awe which fills our hearts when we realise who God is and what he has done for us. It is a love for God which is so great that we would be ashamed to do anything which would displease or grieve him, and makes us happiest when we are doing what pleases him."[3]

---

3. Ferguson, *Grow in Grace*, 29.

Even those who are redeemed may still respond to God out of a servile fear. This will impact our relationship with the Lord, making Him seem distant. We may hesitate to believe what He says and question His love for us. Ferguson says that we need filial fear to drive out servile fear.[4]

Before we go much further, consider the ways in which this might be true for you. Consider whether you might think of God more like an angry earthly father than a perfect and loving Father in heaven who has rescued, redeemed, and adopted you into His family.

Multifaceted Fear

Let's take a look at filial fear a bit more and unpack it. Many Christians summarize the fear of the Lord as reverence or awe. But that's really only part of it. A fear of the Lord encompasses a number of things, including awe, wonder, reverence, worship, adoration, gratitude, love, and obedience. C. H. Spurgeon said that fearing the Lord is shorthand for "expressing real faith, hope, love, holiness of living, and every grace which makes up true godliness."[5] This is really only the beginning of understanding what it means to fear the Lord. We'll continue to explore it in coming chapters. Let's look at a few of those characteristics of filial fear now.

Fear Is Awe and Wonder

When was the last time you saw something truly awesome? The word *awesome* has been overused in recent decades, so

---

4. Ferguson, *Grow in Grace*, 29.

5. C. H. Spurgeon, "Godly Fear and Its Goodly Consequence," Bible Bulletin Board, www.biblebb.com/files/spurgeon/1290.htm.

much so that it has lost its true sense of meaning. The word *awesome* means something that inspires awe, while *awe* is an emotion that combines dread, veneration, and wonder inspired by authority or something sacred.[6] Rather than being used for significant and weighty things, like being astonished at the power of an erupting volcano or standing in the presence of a king, *awesome* is now used more to mean "very good" or "great," as in, "This is an awesome piece of pizza." Interestingly, according to *Merriam Webster*, the word *awe* originally meant "terror" and now means something more like "wonder."[7]

People feel awe in the presence of someone who has the authority to do them harm or good, like a defendant before a judge or a subject before a king. Soldiers in the lowest ranks of the military would feel awe before their commander. We would also feel awe in the midst of a ferocious lightning storm. When the wind howls outside and the power flickers and the lightning cracks, we might look outside the window and marvel at the power of the storm, grateful that we are safe inside.

To stand before something and be filled with wonder is like someone who has lived in the middle of the country and never before seen the ocean. She finally takes a trip to the sea, and her first glimpse of the endless blue water, the feel of the soft sand under her feet, the sound of the powerful waves crashing ashore culminate in a feeling of wonder. She might

---

6. *Merriam Webster*, s.v. "awe (n.)." www.merriam-webster.com/dictionary /awe.

7. *Merriam Webster*, s.v. "awesome (adj.)," www.merriam-webster.com /dictionary/awesome.

feel like the breath has been knocked out of her. She might not want to blink. Her senses might be overcome. Words fail her.

Such awe and wonder is what we have when we fear the Lord. It grows and develops out of being in His presence and knowing who He is in His holiness, magnificence, righteousness, and might—and knowing at the same time we are His beloved.

An example of such awe is Peter's response to the power of Jesus. When Jesus first called the disciples, they were fishing. They had been out all night trying to catch fish but had caught nothing. Then Jesus told them to try again. They did so,

> and when they had done this, they caught a great number of fish, and their net was breaking. So they signaled to their partners in the other boat to come and help them. And they came and filled both the boats, so that they began to sink. When Simon Peter saw it, he fell down at Jesus' knees, saying, "Depart from me, for I am a sinful man, O Lord!"
>
> For he and all who were with him were astonished at the catch of fish which they had taken. (Luke 5:6–9)

In describing this passage, Jerry Bridges remarked, "Peter became acutely and painfully aware of his sinfulness. But what made him fall down before Jesus was not his sin, but Jesus' deity. It was the reaction of the creature to his Creator. It was the profound awe of recognizing the vast difference between himself and the infinite, eternal God."[8]

---

8. Jerry Bridges, *The Joy of Fearing God* (Colorado Springs, Colo.: Water-Brook, 2016), 38.

One of my favorite illustrations of this awe and wonder is from John Piper. He provides an illustration of exploring an unknown glacier in winter:

> Just as you reach a sheer cliff with a spectacular view of miles and miles of jagged ice and mountains of snow, a terrible storm breaks in. The wind is so strong that the fear rises in your heart that it might blow you over the cliff. But in the midst of the storm you discover a cleft in the ice where you can hide. Here you feel secure. But, even though secure, the awesome might of the storm rages on, and you watch it with a kind of trembling pleasure as it surges out across the distant glaciers.

At first there was the fear that this terrible storm and awesome terrain might claim your life. But then you found a refuge and gained the hope that you would be safe. But not everything in the feeling called fear vanished from your heart. Only the life-threatening part. There remained the trembling, the awe, the wonder, the feeling that you would never want to tangle with such a storm or be the adversary of such a power.[9]

> *He shelters us in the shadow of His wings. We are protected from His judgment. The fear of the Lord is our response to being in that place of safety and of knowing we are loved.*

---

9. John Piper, *The Pleasures of God: Meditations on God's Delight in Being God* (Colorado Springs, Colo.: Multnomah, 2012), 186.

Piper likens this to the fear of the Lord: "God's greatness is greater than the universe of stars, and his power is behind the unendurable cold of arctic storms. Yet he cups his hand around us and says, 'Take refuge in my love and let the terrors of my power become the awesome fireworks of your happy night-sky.' The fear of God is what is left of the storm when you have a safe place to watch right in the middle of it."[10]

We know how powerful and mighty and holy God is. We know that the life of everyone on earth is under His control. He is mightier than the storm in the illustration. Yet by His grace He has rescued us from sin and death through the sacrifice of His Son, Jesus Christ. He shelters us in the shadow of His wings. We are protected from His judgment. The fear of the Lord is our response to being in that place of safety and of knowing we are loved.

Fear Is Reverence

I enjoy studying history, and one thing I find especially fascinating is learning about nations that have a monarchy. This is perhaps because it is so foreign to what I am used to, having always lived in a country headed by a president rather than by a king or queen. It's difficult to understand the unique role a monarch has, accompanied by all the pomp and circumstance. Even the expected response subjects give to their monarch is different from how we might respond to a president. There is a deep respect and reverence for what the king or queen symbolizes. The person who is king or queen disappears, and the nation, traditions, laws, and freedoms that

10. Piper, *Pleasures of God*, 187.

they symbolize become paramount. The monarch represents all that the nation and its people are.

When subjects meet with the monarchy, they bow in respect; these days, women curtsy and men bow their head. When subjects leave the presence of a king or queen, they walk out backward rather than turn their back on the monarch. They refer to the monarch as "Your Majesty." They treat their monarch with reverence.

Another aspect to a fear of the Lord is reverence. We respect God for who He is as Creator and Ruler of all things. We respond to Him the way He has prescribed rather than in any flippant way we like. God is God and we are not. We remember that difference in how we approach Him. Yes, He is our Father, but He is unlike any earthly father. Therefore, we show Him respect. We use His name the way He has called us to. We don't treat Him like a Magic 8 Ball or a slot machine, but as the one who created all things. The writer of the book of Hebrews reminds us, "Therefore, since we are receiving a kingdom which cannot be shaken, let us have grace, by which we may serve God acceptably with reverence and godly fear" (12:28).

When we fear the Lord, we don't want to offend or disrespect Him. Therefore, we seek to understand who He is and what He requires of us. We respect His rule and authority in our lives.

In C. S. Lewis's book *The Lion, the Witch and the Wardrobe*, Susan and Lucy ask Mr. and Mrs. Beaver about the lion Aslan, for they were to meet him. He was the true king of Narnia and was revered by the loyal Narnians.

"Is—is he a man?" asked Lucy.

"Aslan a man!" said Mr. Beaver sternly. "Certainly not. I tell you he is the King of the wood and the son of the great Emperor-Beyond-the-Sea. Don't you know who is the King of Beasts? Aslan is a lion—the Lion, *the* great Lion."

"Ooh!" said Susan, "I'd thought he was a man. Is he—quite safe? I shall feel rather nervous about meeting a lion."

"That you will, dearie, and no mistake," said Mrs. Beaver, "if there's anyone who can appear before Aslan without their knees knocking, they're either braver than most or else just silly."

"Then he isn't safe?" asked Lucy.

"Safe?" said Mr. Beaver. "Don't you hear what Mrs. Beaver tells you? Who said anything about safe? 'Course he isn't safe. But he's good. He's the king I tell you."[11]

Fear Is Worship

The apostle John is often referred to as the disciple whom Jesus loved. He was the only apostle who did not die a martyr's death; instead, John was exiled to the island of Patmos. He was sent there as punishment for preaching the gospel. While he was there, he had a vision of heaven and recorded what we now have as the final book in our Bible, Revelation:

> Then I turned to see the voice that spoke with me. And having turned I saw seven golden lampstands, and in the midst of the seven lampstands One like the Son of Man, clothed with a garment down to the feet and

---

11. C. S. Lewis, *The Lion, the Witch and the Wardrobe* (New York: Collier, 1950), 75–76.

girded about the chest with a golden band. His head and hair were white like wool, as white as snow, and His eyes like a flame of fire; His feet were like fine brass, as if refined in a furnace, and His voice as the sound of many waters; He had in His right hand seven stars, out of His mouth went a sharp two-edged sword, and His countenance was like the sun shining in its strength. And when I saw Him, I fell at His feet as dead. But He laid His right hand on me, saying to me, "Do not be afraid; I am the First and the Last. I am He who lives, and was dead, and behold, I am alive forevermore. Amen. And I have the keys of Hades and of Death." (1:12–18)

When we encounter the one true God, we can't help but fall at His feet in worship. It is the right response, for God is worthy. He is the Alpha and the Omega. He is our Maker and Creator. He is the King and Ruler of all. Though John's response is quite dramatic, it does show that fear is worship. When we fear God, we give Him the honor He is due.

> *What makes filial fear different from servile fear is love— the love of a child toward his or her father and the father to the child.*

One of the obvious ways we do this is in our worship with the saints on the Lord's Day. We gather together and sing praises to our great God. We proclaim our faith aloud as we recite creeds and confessions. We pray, hear the word preached, and feast on the Communion meal.

In our day-to-day lives, we worship the Lord in the quiet of our hearts as we honor Him with our lives by trusting and obeying His word. We worship Him as we thank and praise

Him for His generous provisions each day. We worship Him as we turn aside from idols and look to Him alone for life, purpose, and salvation.

To fear the Lord is to worship Him. Let us prostrate our hearts before Him.

Fear Is Love and Adoration

In the beginning of this chapter I asked whether the fear of the Lord is like the terror I felt when I stood at the mountain cliff and looked down. I think in some sense there is a bit of terror, especially when we realize who God is in His power, majesty, and might. Like Mr. Beaver, we understand that God is not safe. But we also know that He is good. As we've seen, there are multiple facets to fearing the Lord. While there is some sense of trepidation, it doesn't remain.

The reason why is love.

What makes filial fear different from servile fear is love—the love of a child toward his or her father and the father to the child. As children love and adore their father and want to please him, we likewise love and are loved by our Father in heaven. We also desire to please Him. As Ferguson writes, "Filial fear, the fear of a son for his Father, is produced by God's love for us. More exactly, it is the result of discovering that the God whom we thought of with slavish, servile fear, the holy, righteous, terrifying God of judgment and majesty, is also the God who forgives us through Jesus Christ."[12] As the psalmist understood,

---

12. Ferguson, *Grow in Grace*, 32.

> If You, LORD, should mark iniquities,
> O Lord, who could stand?
> But there is forgiveness with You,
> That You may be feared. (Ps. 130:3–4)

God's love for us began in eternity past when he chose us in Christ (see Eph. 1:4–5). God loved us first. As we'll see in a later chapter, the more we grow in our understanding of the depths of His love and grace for us in Christ, the more we must respond in love and adoration.

Though we have been forgiven by grace through faith, we still sin. When we do, we don't feel servile fear because we expect punishment; rather, we are saddened by our sin because we love God. We regret what we've done. Our sin has placed a barrier between us and God, creating a kind of relational distance. Through the gospel of grace, we have access to the Father, and we come before Him in repentance. We come in confidence because we are children of the King. And what grace! He has already forgiven us through the shed blood of Christ.

An example of love and the fear of the Lord is the apostle Peter. He was one of Jesus's closest and dearest friends. He was known to be outspoken and often jumped in before thinking. Perhaps because he was an uneducated fisherman, Peter felt the need to prove himself. There's no way to know for certain, but he is depicted in Scripture as saying and doing things out of turn. Peter had difficulty grasping the truth that Jesus would die. On one such occasion, when Jesus told the disciples plainly of His death and resurrection, Peter responded by rebuking Jesus (Mark 8:32), to which Jesus responded,

"Get behind Me, Satan! For you are not mindful of the things of God, but the things of men" (v. 33).

On the night before He was betrayed, Jesus warned Peter that he would deny knowing Him. He told him that Satan "has asked for you, that he may sift you as wheat" (Luke 22:31). But Jesus prayed that Peter's faith would endure and that he would then in turn strengthen the disciples. Peter responded,

> "Lord, I am ready to go with You, both to prison and to death."
> Then [the Lord] said, "I tell you, Peter, the rooster shall not crow this day before you will deny three times that you know Me." (vv. 33–34)

Later that night, Jesus was betrayed and taken away. Peter followed at a safe distance. He waited in the high priest's courtyard to hear news of what was happening. Other people recognized him and asked him if he was one of Jesus's followers. He denied that he was—twice. And then came the third denial:

> Peter said, "Man, I do not know what you are saying!"
> Immediately, while he was still speaking, the rooster crowed. And the Lord turned and looked at Peter. Then Peter remembered the word of the Lord, how He had said to him, "Before the rooster crows, you will deny Me three times." So Peter went out and wept bitterly. (vv. 60–62)

We can only imagine what Peter saw in Jesus's eyes when the Lord turned and looked at him. Perhaps it was a mixture of sadness and love? We do know that Peter remembered the conversation from earlier that night. He must have remembered Jesus telling him that He had already prayed for him. Jesus loved him in that prayer. Perhaps Peter was reminded of that love, and in realizing he failed his Lord, he broke down and wept. This is the response of one who feared the Lord with a filial fear.

In this chapter we began to define, or rather describe, the fear of the Lord. We'll continue to explore this fear more in the next chapter as we look at why we are to fear the Lord.

Chapter 3

FEAR THE LORD
FOR WHO HE IS

Do you know the story behind your name and why it was chosen? Do you know what your name means?

Choosing a name for a child is not as easy as it seems. In our culture, we might name children after a relative, a celebrity, or someone important to us. Or we might choose a name because we like the sound of it. More often than not, we rule out a name because we know someone else by that name. Anyone who is a teacher can attest to this!

My husband and I struggled to find just the right names for our two boys. While there were many girl names that we liked, there were fewer boy names from which to choose. It was a challenge to find one we both liked. In the end, it turns out that our sons' names rhyme—which means neither of them responds when I call for them because they each think I am calling for the other!

In the Bible, the meaning of names is significant. God often instructed prophets to give their children names that reflected what was happening at that time in biblical history. For example, Isaiah is instructed to name his child Maher-Shalal-Hash-Baz, which means, "The spoil speeds, the prey hastens." Isaiah recorded, "Then the LORD said to me, 'Call

his name Maher-Shalal-Hash-Baz; for before the child shall
have knowledge to cry "My father" and "My mother," the
riches of Damascus and the spoil of Samaria will be taken
away before the king of Assyria'" (Isa. 8:3–4). Imagine writing out a name like that in school each day!

God called the prophet Hosea to give his daughter an
unusual name to speak to God's anger for Israel's sins: "Call
her name Lo-Ruhamah, for I will no longer have mercy on
the house of Israel" (Hosea 1:6). Her name literally is "No
Mercy."

Names are also given to describe the character of the
person or who that person would one day be. God changed
Abram's name to Abraham, which means "the father of many
nations" (Gen. 17:5). The angel instructed Joseph to name the
baby Mary would bear Jesus, which means "Savior" (Matt.
1:21). When Jesus first met Peter, his name was Simon, but
the Lord changed it to Peter, meaning "rock" (Matt. 16:18).

In our journey to grow in the fear of the Lord, we need to
know who God is and what He has done. In this chapter, we
are going to explore who God is by looking at His name and
His defining characteristics. Because God is so great, it takes
many names and attributes to describe Him—so many that
we will look at just a few in this chapter.[1] As you read, take
time to focus your heart on what you learn about who God
is. May it help you see God as greater; may it increase your

---

1. A practical way to grow in the fear of the Lord is to study the names,
attributes, and characteristics of God. A few useful books to aid in that study
are John Frame, *The Doctrine of God* (Phillipsburg, N.J.: P&R, 2002); Arthur
Pink, *The Attributes of God* (Grand Rapids: Baker Books, 1975); and J. I. Packer,
Knowing God (Downers Grove, Ill.: InterVasity, 1973).

awe, wonder, reverence, worship, and love for the One who loved you first.

The Great I AM

When Moses first met God, it was nothing less than an awesome experience—in the true sense of the word. He had been tending his father-in-law's flock when he came to Horeb, the mountain of God. There, an angel of the Lord appeared to him in a burning bush. Imagine witnessing a bush burn without being consumed! Moses stopped to watch this curious anomaly.

God called to him out of the bush and said, "Do not draw near this place. Take your sandals off your feet, for the place where you stand is holy ground" (Ex. 3:5). God then introduced Himself as the covenant-keeping God of Abraham, Isaac, and Jacob. Moses responded by hiding his face in fear. God then told him He had heard the plight of His people, and He had come to deliver them. He would send Moses to release His people from slavery in Egypt.

Moses then asked, "Indeed, when I come to the children of Israel and say to them, 'The God of your fathers has sent me to you,' and they say to me, 'What is His name?' what shall I say to them?" (Ex. 3:13).

God responded, "I AM WHO I AM" (v. 14). He then said, "Thus you shall say to the children of Israel, 'I AM has sent me to you.' Moreover God said to Moses, 'Thus you shall say to the children of Israel: "The LORD God of your

> *Most assuredly, I say to you, before Abraham was, I AM. (John 8:58)*

fathers, the God of Abraham, the God of Isaac, and the God of Jacob, has sent me to you. This is My name forever, and this is My memorial to all generations"'" (vv. 14–15).

God defined for Moses who He is: the great I AM. He first used the name I AM WHO I AM (or "I will be what I will be"), then He shortened it to I AM, and finally He used the name Lord. In Hebrew this name is Yahweh, and it sounds like a form of the Hebrew verb "to be."[2] In our Bibles it is often written as LORD, with all capital letters. It's the most common name for God in the Bible. The Jews had such a reverence and respect for this name that they refused to say it out loud; instead, they used the name Adonai (Lord), which is not a name, but the title "sovereign one."[3]

Scholars debate the exact meaning of this name and, as a result, suggest several nuances. In using this name, God was teaching Moses that He has always existed and is not dependent on anyone; God is not created and does not rely on anything outside of Him to sustain Him. Theologians use the word *aseity* to describe the truth that God is the first cause; He is self-existent, self-sustaining, and autonomous. God's name also tells us that He is unchangeable; He always was and always will be. He is the same yesterday, today, and for all eternity (Heb. 13:8). And this name told Moses that God would be present with His people as Moses led them out of slavery, which was central to what lay ahead for God's people.

Throughout the rest of Scripture, the name I AM is used in multiple contexts, describing God's eternal existence, His control over all things, His acts of salvation and redemption,

2. Frame, *Doctrine of God*, chap. 2, Kindle.

3. R. C. Sproul, *The Holiness of God* (Carol Stream, Ill.: Tyndale, 1998), 18.

and His covenantal presence with His people. This is the name Jesus used in responding to the Jews in John 8:58: "Most assuredly, I say to you, before Abraham was, I AM."

Knowing God as Lord; as I AM; as the always existent, unchangeable Almighty One is foundational as we begin to explore who God is. This name sets Him apart from all other gods. John Calvin wrote that we must know this name and its meaning, "that our minds may be filled with admiration as often as his incomprehensible essence is mentioned."[4] And may it help us understand the characteristics we will look at in this chapter.

God's Holiness

One of the hymns I grew up singing in church was "Holy, Holy, Holy":

> Holy, holy, holy! Lord God Almighty!
> Early in the morning our song shall rise to Thee;
> Holy, holy, holy, merciful and mighty!
> God in three Persons, blessed Trinity!

These hymn lyrics are an echo of a similar song in the book of Isaiah, when the prophet was given a vision of heaven. In Isaiah 6 we read an account of Isaiah standing before the throne of God. He saw the Lord seated high on His throne, and above the throne stood seraphim. The Bible tells us that His robe filled the temple. Imagine how grand and imposing! The seraphim had six wings, four of which they

---

4. John Calvin, *Commentary on Exodus*, https://biblehub.com/commentaries/calvin/exodus/3.htm.

used to cover their faces and feet. They flew around, crying to one another, "Holy, holy, holy is the LORD of hosts; the whole earth is full of His glory!" (v. 3). The doorposts then shook, and the temple filled with smoke. In response to what he saw, heard, and felt, Isaiah said,

> Woe is me, for I am undone!
> Because I am a man of unclean lips,
> And I dwell in the midst of a people of unclean lips;
> For my eyes have seen the King,
> The LORD of hosts. (v. 5)

What an extraordinary experience and response! Isaiah saw created beings who, though they were not sinful, could not look at the face of God, so they covered their own faces as they hovered above the throne. He saw the great I AM, beheld the holiness of God, and saw himself in stark contrast. While Isaiah was a prophet and a righteous man, as he stood before the throne of God, he saw his true nature. He saw himself in his fallen human state, and all he could do was say, "Woe is me!" As R. C. Sproul wrote, "In that single moment, all of his self-esteem was shattered. In a brief second he was exposed, made naked beneath the gaze of the absolute standard of holiness."[5]

As mentioned before, the Bible describes many characteristics of God. We know that God is merciful, just, good, kind, and loving, among others. But only one characteristic is listed three times in a row: God's holiness. Sproul wrote that such repetition in Scripture means "to elevate it to the superlative

---

5. Sproul, *Holiness of God*, 28.

degree, to attach to it emphasis of superimportance."[6] We could compare it to the way we use exclamation points to emphasize a point or in modern-day parlance, an emoji to express strong emotion. When the Bible tells us God is thrice holy, we need to stop and pay attention. It is telling us that God is above and beyond anything else our minds can fathom.

What does it mean when the Bible says that God is holy? The word *holiness* means "to be separate," or "set apart." Many things in Scripture are described as holy, including objects used for worship at the temple. They were set apart from the whole for special use. God's people are called to be holy, set apart from the world. God is certainly holy in that He is separate and apart from anything else, for there is none like Him. But it also means more than that.

> When the Bible tells us God is thrice holy, we need to stop and pay attention. It is telling us that God is above and beyond anything else our minds can fathom.

In *The Holiness of God*, R. C. Sproul says that holiness contains not only set apart-ness but also includes purity, transcendence, and mystery. He wrote, "When the Bible calls God holy, it means primarily that God is transcendentally separate. He is so far above and beyond us that He seems almost totally foreign to us."[7] Holiness includes God's moral purity; He is not tainted by even a shadow of sin. As John wrote, "God is light and in Him is no darkness at all" (1 John 1:5). In describing God's holiness, Arthur Pink wrote,

---

7. Sproul, *Holiness of God*, 36.

"As God's power is the opposite of the native weakness of the creature, as His wisdom is in complete contrast from the least defect of understanding or folly, so His holiness is the very antithesis of all moral blemish or defilement."[8]

Holiness is not merely one of God's attributes in a list, right alongside things like kindness, justice, and truth; rather, holiness is essential and inherent to who God is. God is holy. Therefore, His wisdom is holy, His justice is holy, His power is holy. He is far beyond anything that we know here on earth. In Isaiah, God, the Holy One, asked, "'To whom then will you liken Me, or to whom shall I be equal?'" (Isa. 40:25).

The twentieth-century German scholar Rudolph Otto studied how people respond when they experience the holy. He used the term *numinous* to describe their encounter, which means "divine power."[9] Otto characterized a person's response to the numinous as a sense of "awfulness" (being filled with awe) or, as we are exploring in this book, a holy fear of the Lord.[10] It's the experience of coming face-to-face with One who is wholly other. It's being overwhelmed before the majestic and transcendent. It's realizing your insignificance before the all-glorious One. It's having a profound sense of yourself as creature and God as God. It is being wonder struck that One so holy and glorious would welcome you into His presence.

---

8. Pink, *Attributes of God*, 41.

9. Gene Veith, "The Numinous," *Cranach* (blog), *Patheos*, June 4, 2013, www.patheos.com/blogs/geneveith/2013/06/the-numinous/.

10. Clara Sarrocco, "Surprised by Awe: C. S. Lewis and Rudolf Otto's *The Idea of the Holy*," *Touchstone*, May/June 2011, www.touchstonemag.com/archives/article.php?id=24–03–036-f.

This is why when both Isaiah and the apostle John (in the book of Revelation) had a vision of God in heaven, they responded in such profound ways. John fell down as though dead, and Isaiah cried out, "Woe is me!" And this is why we are called to a greater fear, the fear of the Lord. Because God is holy, because He is indescribably transcendent, our only response is that of awe, reverence, wonder, and worship. The psalmist recognized this truth in Psalm 99:5:

> Exalt the LORD our God,
> And worship at His footstool—
> He is holy.

God's Goodness

How do we usually respond when someone asks, "How are you?"

Most often we reply, "I am good." It's a common response. *Good* is a word we use to describe anything from the food we ate to the movie we watched to a sermon we heard. We use it to express that we liked or enjoyed something. We use it to say we approve of something or that it is the right fit for our needs. If we were to put the word *good* on a scale, it would be on the low end from words like *better* and *best*.

These aren't necessarily wrong uses for the word, but in using it to describe the hamburger we ate yesterday, it loses its significance when we open our Bibles and read that God is good or when we describe someone as a "good person" because they paid for someone's coffee in the car behind them in the drive-through line. That's because when the Bible describes God as good, it is linked to His very nature.

After Moses's extraordinary experience with the burning bush, God used him to deliver His people from slavery. Moses witnessed more of God's power and might through the ten plagues. He saw God carve a way through the sea for the people to walk through to the other side. He met God on the mountain and received the Ten Commandments. Then in Exodus 33, Moses asked to see God's glory. He wanted to see God face-to-face.

But because God is holy, no one can see His face and live (Ex. 33:20). Instead, God told Moses he could hide behind a rock and watch Him pass by. As He did so, He gave Moses a further description of His character:

> Now the LORD descended in the cloud and stood with him there, and proclaimed the name of the LORD. And the LORD passed before him and proclaimed, "The LORD, the LORD God, merciful and gracious, longsuffering, and abounding in goodness and truth, keeping mercy for thousands, forgiving iniquity and transgression and sin, by no means clearing the guilty, visiting the iniquity of the fathers upon the children and the children's children to the third and the fourth generation." (Ex. 34:5–7)

Again, God used His name I AM and described to Moses who He is and how He acts. Among these characteristics is God's goodness. He abounds in goodness. In the Bible, goodness has to do with perfection and righteousness. This is a characteristic of God repeated throughout Scripture and is inherent to His holiness. The psalmist wrote, "You are good, and do good" (Ps. 119:68). As Pink observed, "There is such an absolute perfection in God's nature and being that nothing is wanting to it or defective in it, and nothing can be added to it to make it better."[11] He is wholly good.

It's difficult to comprehend something that is so perfect that it can't be improved in any way. In our own lives and world, there's always room for improvement. We always seek ways to make technology better. We train our bodies and minds to perform better and to achieve more. But God is perfectly and completely good; it is impossible to add to His goodness.

We often look at things people do and label them as "good." We talk about doing good works such as helping the weak or standing up for what is right. Yet in comparison to God's goodness, our good deeds are as filthy rags (Isa. 64:6). That's because even our motives are tainted by sin.

Because God is perfect and wholly good, He cannot do anything that is *not* good. All His ways are good. From the world that He created

> *While the people and circumstances we meet in this fallen world are not good, we have a good God who rules over it all. We can remind ourselves of His goodness when we face fearful circumstances—when the future ahead seems dark and bleak.*

to His acts in history, from His perfect plan for our lives to His kindness poured out on us in Christ—all that He does is good. The Song of Moses sets forth this truth:

---

11. Pink, *Attributes of God*, 57.

> He is the Rock, His work is perfect;
> For all His ways are justice,
> A God of truth and without injustice;
> Righteous and upright is He. (Deut. 32:4)

Not only is God good and all that He does is good, but also all good things come from God, according to James: "Every good gift and every perfect gift is from above, and comes down from the Father of lights, with whom there is no variation or shadow of turning" (James 1:17). God is the Father of lights. In spiritual terms, darkness implies evil, and there is no darkness in God. He is the source of all that is good, and everything He gives us is good. This verse also tells us that God never changes; there is no "variation or shadow of turning." Our God will never show goodness toward us and then change His mind. We can trust that His goodness toward us will never change.

God's goodness is an important characteristic for fearful hearts. While the people and circumstances we meet in this fallen world are not good, we have a good God who rules over it all. We can remind ourselves of His goodness when we face fearful circumstances—when the future ahead seems dark and bleak. Because God is good, we can trust Him to be with us, to provide for us, to save us. We can expect good things from our good God.

When we consider and dwell on the goodness of God, we respond with holy fear, as the psalmist calls us to:

> Enter into His gates with thanksgiving,
> And into His courts with praise.
> Be thankful to Him, and bless His name.
> For the LORD is good;

His mercy is everlasting,
And His truth endures to all generations.
　(Ps. 100:4–5)

God's Love

Every February I pick up a bag of those heart-shaped candies with words of affection stamped on them—like "True Love" and "Be Mine." I pour them into a bowl, and over the course of a few days, my family gobbles them up, a handful at a time.

It's interesting how a concept like love can be reduced to phrases like "sure love" and "one and only." This is true on February 14, but it's also true in the movies we watch and the music we listen to, in which love is reduced to a feeling that comes and goes with the tide of desire. The definition of love in our culture stands in stark contrast to the love we read about in the Bible, which is not about feelings but about actions; not about ourselves but about others; not about gaining something but about losing everything—and ultimately glorifies not ourselves but the One who loved us first.

The apostle John wrote about love in one of his letters:

Beloved, let us love one another, for love is of God; and everyone who loves is born of God and knows God. He who does not love does not know God, for God is love. In this the love of God was manifested toward us, that God has sent His only begotten Son into the world, that we might live through Him. In this is love, not that we loved God, but that He loved us and sent His Son to be the propitiation for our sins. Beloved, if God so loved us, we also ought to love one another. (1 John 4:7–11)

This passage tells us something else about God and His character: *God is love.*

In this letter, John gave his readers a number of tests to help them measure their faith. Were they in Christ or not? One of those tests was love. John wrote that if we don't love others, we don't know God, for God is love. To know God is to know His love.

Love is such an integral part of God's character that all He does is out of that love. The apostle Paul described what love looks like in 1 Corinthians 13. Love is revealed in actions such as patience and kindness; it doesn't envy or boast; it is not rude or irritable or resentful. We often look at this passage to learn how we are to love others, which is a good thing. Yet this passage also points to God and His love for us. The ultimate act of God's love was seen on the cross, where the Son of God gave His life as a ransom for many, as John points out: "By this we know love, because He laid down His life for us. And we also ought to lay down our lives for the brethren" (1 John 3:16).

First John 4 also teaches us that love originates in our triune God. God the Father, God the Son, and God the Holy Spirit have lived together in perfect and mutual love, joy, and unity from all eternity past (John 17:24). Love begins with God. We wouldn't love had He not loved us first (1 John 4:19). God chose us in love before the foundation of the world to be His own, to be adopted as His sons and daughters (Eph. 1:4). God didn't love us because we were loveable; He chose to love us. He set His love on us and saved us through the blood of His Son.

John's statement "God is love" is sometimes used to claim that God overlooks human sin. The thinking goes that because the Bible says God is love, He must love and accept everyone, and therefore He doesn't hold sinners to account for their actions. Sometimes people misread this statement and believe that love and God are the same thing. Both misrepresentations fail to account for the entirety of the Bible. When we read Scripture, we clearly see that He does not overlook sin; rather, He intervenes to rescue us from it. God's love doesn't leave us as we are; He changes us to become what we were created to be. His love is active, redeeming, and sacrificial. God is also more than just love. As we've studied so far, He is also eternal, transcendent, holy, righteous, and good.

God's love for us is what changes servile fear to filial fear. Because He loved us and made us His own, we don't fear Him as those outside of Christ would; we fear Him with a holy fear—a fear that is awed and filled with wonder at His love for us; a fear that responds with gratitude and love of our own; a fear that exalts and praises His great name.

> *God's love for us is what changes servile fear to filial fear. Because He loved us and made us His own, we don't fear Him as those outside of Christ would; we fear Him with a holy fear—a fear that is awed and filled with wonder at His love for us.*

God's Sovereignty

God's sovereignty is a characteristic laced throughout Scripture. To be *sovereign* means "to have absolute power and authority." The United States is a sovereign nation because it governs itself apart from any other foreign power. In countries that have a monarchy, the king or queen is the sovereign ruler. The Bible teaches us that God is the supreme and ultimate Sovereign over all things. He rules over the cosmos and over every living thing, as the psalmist explained: "The LORD has established His throne in heaven, and His kingdom rules over all" (Ps. 103:19).

The Bible teaches us that God rules over all—both the big and the small. There is no one and nothing outside His sovereign control.

He is sovereign over creation:

He gives snow like wool;
He scatters the frost like ashes;
He casts out His hail like morsels;
Who can stand before His cold?
He sends out His word and melts them;
He causes His wind to blow, and the waters flow.
   (Ps. 147:16–18)

He made the Pleiades and Orion;
He turns the shadow of death into morning
And makes the day dark as night;
He calls for the waters of the sea
And pours them out on the face of the earth;
The LORD is His name. (Amos 5:8)

He is sovereign over the affairs of humankind:

The king's heart is in the hand of the LORD,
Like the rivers of water;
He turns it wherever He wishes. (Prov. 21:1)

A man's heart plans his way, but the LORD directs his steps. (Prov. 16:9)

He is sovereign over things we often attribute to chance or to nature:

> The lot is cast into the lap, but its every decision is from the LORD. (Prov. 16:33)

> I form the light and create darkness,
> I make peace and create calamity;
> I, the LORD, do all these things. (Isa. 45:7)

He is sovereign over every aspect of our salvation:

> Whom He predestined, these He also called; whom He called, these He also justified; and whom He justified, these He also glorified. (Rom. 8:30)

> May the God of all grace, who called us to His eternal glory by Christ Jesus, after you have suffered a while, perfect, establish, strengthen, and settle you. (1 Peter 5:10)

God doesn't just know about the circumstances of our lives; He rules over and governs them. He determines and wills all the events that take place in our lives, both the significant and seemingly insignificant. Not even a hair can fall from our heads without God willing it to do so. As C. H. Spurgeon wrote, "I believe that every particle of dust that dances in the sunbeam does not move an atom more or less than God wishes."[12]

---

12. C. H. Spurgeon, "God's Providence," in *Spurgeon's Sermons*, vol. 54, 1908, Christian Classics Ethereal Library, https://www.ccel.org/ccel/spurgeon/sermons54.xlii.html.

As believers, we don't dispute that God rules over all. Some of us just may have difficulty trusting in His rule. This can happen when we look at His sovereignty as separate from His other characteristics. It's important to know that God's sovereignty doesn't exist in isolation; it is fundamentally linked with who He is in His omniscience, omnipotence, holiness, goodness, and love, among other characteristics. When we remember that God is holy and righteous—that all He does is perfect, good, and right—then we know He will govern and rule out of that righteousness. When we remember that God loved us in Christ before the foundation of the world, we know that the circumstances He brings into our lives are ordered out of that love.

What might all this have to do with our fears and replacing them with a fear of the Lord? Because God is sovereign, He is never caught off guard by the circumstances of our life. He not only knows about the fearful situations we face, but He purposed them to take place and rules over them. Nothing happens in our life outside of His control. It is a comfort to know that an event that catches us by surprise is not a surprise to God. He governs everything from the traffic we sat in that made us late to work to the flu virus our child caught at school. He rules over the tornado that threatened our neighborhood and the company whose stock we invested in that crashed. He allows trials and heartaches and painful situations to cut into our lives and rules over them so that all things work together for our ultimate good and His glory: "And we know that all things work together for good to those who love God, to those who are the called according to His purpose" (Rom. 8:28).

The doctrine of God's sovereignty can be a great comfort for fearful hearts. It causes us to remember God is greater than anything else we fear. When we rest in God's sovereign care for us and trust that He has a good purpose for all that comes our way, we can face fearful circumstances without despair and with hope. When we find ourselves fearful, we can whisper this truth to our hearts: "God is not surprised by this." He knows what is happening. He knows how we feel. He knows just what we need

> *It is a comfort to know that an event that catches us by surprise is not a surprise to God.*

in that moment. We can turn to Him for help and rescue and know that He cares for us. Because He rules over all things, He alone can deliver us. The psalmist reminds us, "God is our refuge and strength, a very present help in trouble" (Ps. 46:1). We can exchange our fears for a holy fear of our sovereign God.

As we dwell on who God is, we see with greater clarity why we are to fear Him. Our sovereign God is the great I AM. He is holy, good, and loving. He rules over all that we fear. He is greater. We can trust Him.

Chapter 4

FEAR THE LORD FOR WHAT HE HAS DONE

What's the best gift you've ever received? Perhaps it was your first bike, complete with a wire basket and plastic fringe hanging from the handles. Or maybe it was the popular doll all your friends had, the one that came with a matching dress for you to wear. Or maybe it was a tree house you and your dad built together in the backyard, where you spent countless afternoons pretending it was a medieval castle, defending it from invading marauders. Or maybe the best gift was an experience, like your first trip to Disney World, where you saw Cinderella's castle, ate Mickey ears ice cream, and rode on Dumbo.

We all love to receive gifts, and when we receive a gift we've always wanted, we remember long after. But what if someone handed you a paper-wrapped package on your birthday and, as you opened it, said, "Now, you'll have to pay me back for this" and then proceeded to hand you the receipt. It would then cease to be a gift, wouldn't it? Because if you worked for it or paid for it or earned it in some way, it is not a gift at all.

In the last chapter, we looked at various reasons to fear the Lord, specifically because of who God is. In this chapter we'll explore additional reasons to fear the Lord: because of what He has done. More specifically, we will focus on some of the gifts He's given us.

The Gift of Creation

I grew up in the mid-Atlantic area of the United States, a region comprised of coastal plains to the east, piedmont further inland, and then mountain ranges in the west. My family and I spent many a weekend or summer vacation in the Appalachian mountain chain of Virginia and Maryland. I loved exploring the densely wooded trails and waterfalls, hiking to the top and seeing the valley stretched out far below. Yet the Appalachians are rather diminutive; the highest peaks are less than seven thousand feet. Compared to other ranges in the United States and even around the world, they are more like rolling hills.

When I was sixteen, I joined a group of friends from my church on a road trip, driving from the east coast to the Rocky Mountains in Colorado. We drove for hours and hours from the suburbs of Washington, D.C., past small towns and large cities, through the plains and sprawling farms of the Midwest, until finally, out of nowhere, rocky peaks jutted out from the flat pasture that had been our roadside companion for what seemed like days. We were almost there, or so I thought.

It still took hours to get there. Even though the mountains' jagged peaks seemed so magnificent from our position on the road, we still had a way to go. And when we did arrive, I had no words. I was speechless, awestruck by the peaks' sheer height, covered in snow even in late July. It was the grandest thing I had seen in my life.

Since then, I've seen more of this beautiful world. I've snorkeled in the teal-blue waters of the tropics and come face-to-face with sea creatures that returned my wide-eyed gaze with one of their own. I've heard the roar of glaciers calving, dropping huge chunks of ice into the frigid Arctic waters. I've marveled at the life that grows and thrives even in the desert, from the blooming cactus to the scampering chipmunk. And in all of it, I see the handiwork of God, our Creator.

The Bible begins with these remarkable words: "In the beginning God created the heavens and the earth" (Gen. 1:1). Over a period of six days, God merely spoke, and everything appeared at the sound of His voice: trees and plants, stars and moons, lions and bears, dolphins and pelicans. God crafted every living thing. He then made man from the dust of the earth, breathed into him the breath of life, and called him Adam. Because it wasn't good for Adam to be alone, God created woman from Adam's side, and she was called Eve.

This great, big, beautiful world exists because God called it into being. He is the Creator; we are His creatures. He is the source and wellspring of all life. He gives us life, breath, and everything else (Acts 17:25). He sends the rains that help the earth produce food for us to eat. He provides for His creatures, great and small. All creation is dependent on His sustaining grace.

> *The Bible tells us that the marvels of this world point to who God is.*

The Bible tells us that the marvels of this world point to who God is: "For since the creation of the world His invisible attributes are clearly seen, being understood by the things that are made, even His eternal power and Godhead, so that they are without excuse" (Rom. 1:20). Everything proclaims God's glory—even the stars sing God's praise. When we look at the roaring ocean as it spits and foams on the shore, we see God's power on display. When we see a field of flowers dressed in finery and brilliant in color, we witness God's creative wonder. When we hold a newborn baby and count each tiny finger and toe, we are astonished at the kindness of God to bring forth such a miracle.

We fear God because He has created all things. He sustains all things. We wake up each morning because He has given us breath for another day. As J. I. Packer noted, "Realizing our moment-by-moment dependence on God the Creator for our very existence makes it appropriate to live lives of devotion, commitment, gratitude, and loyalty toward him, and scandalous not to."[1]

Job was a man who feared God, and his response to all that he lost reflected that. Yet there was more for him to learn about God. At the end of the book of Job, when God finally spoke to Job in the whirlwind, He taught Job more of what it means to fear Him. He did so by pointing to His works of creation and His providential care over all He has made. God asked Job a series of questions (several chapters' worth!) to show him that God is God and he was not:

> "Have you commanded the morning since your days began, and caused the dawn to know its place…?

---

1. Packer, *Concise Theology*, 22.

"Can you lift up your voice to the clouds,
That an abundance of water may cover you?
Can you send out lightnings, that they may go,
And say to you, 'Here we are!'?...

"Who provides food for the raven,
When its young ones cry to God,
And wander about for lack of food?...

"Have you given the horse strength?
Have you clothed his neck with thunder?"
    (Job 38:12, 34–35, 41; 39:19)

When God finished speaking, Job then responded,

"I know that You can do everything,
And that no purpose of Yours can be withheld from You.
You asked, 'Who is this who hides counsel without
    knowledge?'
Therefore I have uttered what I did not understand,
Things too wonderful for me, which I did not know....

"I have heard of You by the hearing of the ear,
But now my eye sees You.
Therefore I abhor myself,
And repent in dust and ashes."
    (Job 42:2–3, 5–6)

Job encountered God and saw Him as creator and sustainer of all things, as the sovereign one who governs over all. Like Isaiah, he saw himself in contrast and could only respond with a holy fear.

Pause today to marvel at all God has made. Praise Him for the gift of life each day.

The Gift of Immanuel

As we saw in the last chapter, the most common name for God is Yahweh, or I AM. We learned of its meaning and significance throughout Scripture. We learned that it is used to describe God's presence with His people, His covenant commitment to be our God and dwell among us.

What is striking is that the great I AM—the One who has no beginning or end, the One who flung the stars in the sky, the One who is surrounded by creatures who cannot look on His face, the One who could not let Moses see His face and live—wrapped Himself in human flesh and dwelt among us: "And the Word became flesh and dwelt among us, and we beheld His glory, the glory as of the only begotten of the Father, full of grace and truth" (John 1:14). God incarnated as a human baby, woven in the womb and born of the virgin Mary.

The incarnation is a wondrous act that, when considered, brings forth awe and wonder. Jesus Christ is the second person of the Trinity, equal with the Father and the Holy Spirit. He always is and always was. He was there before time began, when He and the Father determined to save His people from their sins. He was there at creation, when our triune God brought life into being. Paul tells us in Philippians 2 that Jesus did not consider that equality something to cling to, as a reason not to serve, but He left the halls of heaven to come to earth and took the form of a servant. He entered this world not as a king but as a baby. He lived not in a palace but in a village as a carpenter's son. As Isaiah described Him:

> He is despised and rejected by men,
> A Man of sorrows and acquainted with grief.

And we hid, as it were, our faces from Him;
He was despised, and we did not esteem Him.
(Isa. 53:3)

In the incarnation, Jesus did not give up His deity, for He was fully God and fully man. As the God-man, Jesus could do what we could not do: obey the law of God. And in so doing, He became the perfect sacrifice for our sin: "He made Him who knew no sin to be sin for us, that we might become the righteousness of God in Him" (2 Cor. 5:21).

The incarnation was the only way to rescue and redeem us. It was the only way to bring us back into the presence of God. It was the only way to make us His own. What wonder! What a miracle! What mystery! As John Calvin wrote:

> It was his task to swallow up death. Who but the Life could do this? It was his task to conquer sin. Who but very Righteousness could do this? It was his task to rout the powers of world and air. Who but a power higher than world and air could do this? Now where does life or righteousness, or lordship and authority of heaven lie but with God alone? Therefore our most merciful God, when he willed that we be redeemed, made himself our Redeemer in the person of his only-begotten Son.[2]

What's even more amazing is that Jesus Christ reigns in heaven in His resurrected body. He remains enfleshed. Consider the significance that God would not only incarnate to

---

2. John Calvin, *The Institutes of the Christian Religion* (Philadelphia: Westminster Press, 1960), 2.12.3.

live and die for us but that He would remain the God-man for eternity—scars and all.

Take time today to pause and dwell on what it means that God became flesh for you.

God's Gift of Grace

John Newton was an eighteenth-century pastor who influenced William Wilberforce and the Abolitionist movement in England. Most people who are familiar with Newton know him for his well-loved hymn "Amazing Grace." We recognize that this hymn is so remarkable when we consider Newton's life prior to faith in Christ.

> *Consider the significance that God would not only incarnate to live and die for us but that He would remain the God-man for eternity—scars and all.*

John Newton's father was a sailor, and John followed in his father's footsteps at a young age. He spent his adolescence on his father's ship and, during breaks away from sailing, lived a wild and raucous life. At one point, he found himself forced into service in the British navy, where severe discipline was the norm. He was later dismissed because he just wouldn't cooperate and follow the rules.[3] He then returned to the life of a sailor and became involved in the slave trade. Newton's life became increasingly rough and out of control—until he nearly died.

---

3. Stephen J. Nichols, "The Life of John Newton," July 3, 2018, in *5 Minutes in Church History* (podcast), www.5minutesinchurchhistory.com/the -life-of-john-newton/.

Like many sailors in his day, Newton endured a shipwreck in which he almost lost his life. In March of 1748, he was on the ship *Greyhound* when a terrible storm arose at sea. He was asleep when water burst through the wall of his cabin and woke him up. He and the other sailors spent all night trying to keep the boat from sinking. During this event he prayed, "Lord, have mercy!"[4] From that point on, he became serious about his faith, though it was some time before he was convicted of the evils of the slave trade.

At twenty-nine he had a stroke, which ended his days on the sea. He then came to know the revivalist preachers Whitefield and Wesley and attended their evangelical gatherings. He studied Scripture and grew in his faith. In his thirties, he followed the call to the pastorate.

For Newton, the more he grew in his faith, the more he realized the depths of his sin and depravity. The more he learned about who God is and what He has done, the more he saw his desperate need for grace—and the more he responded with awe, wonder, and worship.

The next work of God I want us to focus on is God's gift of grace to us in Christ. *Grace* is a word many people use—both inside and outside of Christianity. Some use it to mean giving ourselves or someone else a pass, as in "I need to give myself grace; I can't expect to get everything right." We might use it to mean kindness or compassion. But it's only when we encounter the gospel of grace as found in the Bible that we can proclaim with Newton, "Amazing grace! how sweet the sound that saved a wretch like me!"

---

4. Nichols, "Life of John Newton."

God's grace is deeper and more immense than we realize. Its significance is immeasurable. It is shocking and outrageous. There's nothing in this world that compares to it. Surely it will take an eternity to plumb the depths of what God's grace means for us.

In theological terms, grace is often summarized as unmerited favor. It is God's kindness we haven't earned. God shows this kindness in the gift of eternal life through faith in Jesus Christ. Yet such grace is also demerited favor. It's not only that we haven't earned God's favor; we don't even deserve it. We are born in sin and thus deserve God's wrath and eternal damnation. Arthur Pink defined God's grace this way: "Divine grace is the sovereign and saving favor of God exercised in the bestowment of blessings upon those who have no merit in them and for which no compensation is demanded from them…. It is completely unmerited and unsought, and is altogether unattracted by anything in or from or by the objects upon which it is bestowed."[5] When we trace God's grace in Scripture, we see that it is woven throughout our salvation.

God's grace awakens us from death to life. God's grace for us began in eternity past when He chose us in Christ to be adopted into the family of God (Eph. 1:4–5). By His grace, He awakens us from spiritual death and gives us new life. Apart from this grace, we could not respond to the call of the gospel with faith, for we were dead in our trespasses and sins (Eph. 2:1–6).

---

5. Pink, *Attributes of God*, 66.

God's grace saves us. We are saved by grace through faith. Salvation is God's work in us; it isn't our own work, for we cannot save ourselves. Faith itself is a gift of God and the means by which we are justified (Eph. 2:8). As Sproul noted, "Unless we are born of the Spirit of God, unless God sheds His holy love in our hearts, unless He stoops in His grace to change our hearts, we will not love Him. He is the One who takes the initiative to restore our souls."[6]

God's grace teaches and trains us. Upon salvation, God does not leave us in our sin. He forgives our sin because of the sacrifice of Christ on our behalf and accepts Christ's perfect life lived for us. But He doesn't overlook our sin or leave us there to continue in it. Rather, He trains us by His grace to put off sin and put on godliness. Paul explained this in his letter to Titus: "For the grace of God that brings salvation has appeared to all men, teaching us that, denying ungodliness and worldly lusts, we should live soberly, righteously, and godly in the present age, looking for the blessed hope and glorious appearing of our great God and Savior Jesus Christ, who gave Himself for us, that He might redeem us from every lawless deed and purify for Himself His own special people, zealous for good works" (Titus 2:11–14).

> *From beginning to end, all is of God's grace. We don't deserve it; we haven't earned it.*

God's grace sanctifies and transforms us. By His grace, God changes and transforms us into the likeness of His Son, Jesus Christ. Paul speaks

---

6. Sproul, *Holiness of God*, 180.

to this grace at work in his own life: "By the grace of God I am what I am, and His grace toward me was not in vain; but I labored more abundantly than they all, yet not I, but the grace of God which was with me" (1 Cor. 15:10). We are called to yield to the work God does within us and to participate in it, knowing that as we work out our salvation, it is God who is at work (Phil. 2:12–13).

God's grace makes us new. By His grace, God will finish the work He began in us; He has promised to complete the work of making us new. We can trust that He will strengthen, sustain, and preserve us to the end when we meet our Savior in glory. We will be transformed and stand blameless before Him, "being confident of this very thing, that He who has begun a good work in you will complete it until the day of Jesus Christ" (Phil. 1:6).

From beginning to end, all is of God's grace. We don't deserve it; we haven't earned it. John Newton knew this first-hand. That's why he wrote, "'Twas grace that taught my heart to fear, and grace my fears relieved." That's what makes grace so amazing! Wouldn't you agree?

The Gift of the Spirit

Imagine a distant relative has passed away, and you have inherited an heirloom. It is a valuable heirloom, both monetarily and historically. But to you, it is just another object to collect dust. You shove it into a drawer somewhere and forget about it, only to learn later of its history and importance to your family—and of its monetary value.

One of God's gifts to us is often overlooked or minimized—taken for granted and set somewhere on a shelf to be considered only on occasion. But this gift is powerful. It is as essential to our faith as breath is to our lungs. In fact, it is the active force behind life, faith, and the word of God. What gift is this? *The gift of the Holy Spirit.*

On the night before He was betrayed, Jesus dined with His disciples one last time. He gave a talk called the Upper Room Discourse, in which He taught them about their vital union with Him, what would happen when He left, and why He needed to go. The apostle John records this discourse in John 14–17, where we find Jesus promising that the Holy Spirit would come.

Jesus told them, "I will pray the Father, and He will give you another Helper, that He may abide with you forever" (John 14:16). This word *helper* is *paraklétos* in Greek.[7] It means "comforter" or "advocate, someone who comes to one's aid." It was often used in legal contexts to describe a lawyer, one who interceded to a judge on behalf of another. We find another form of this word, *parakaleó,* in New Testament passages that describe the comfort and encouragement God gives to us and that we likewise give to one another.

The Holy Spirit is the third person of the Trinity, coequal with the Father and the Son. He too was there at creation, hovering across the waters of a world yet to be formed. In fact, He was the agent of creation; it was His power and energy that brought forth all we see.[8] The Spirit is also the

7. *Strong's Concordance*, s.v. "*paraklétos*," https://biblehub.com/greek/3875 .htm.

8. Alistair Begg, "Five Truths about the Holy Spirit," *Ligonier Blog*, Ligonier Ministries, January 31, 2020, www.ligonier.org/blog/five-truths-about -holy-spirit/.

agent who carried out our new birth in Christ: "not by works of righteousness which we have done, but according to His mercy He saved us, through the washing of regeneration and renewing of the Holy Spirit" (Titus 3:5).

It is the Spirit who brought our dead hearts to life so we could respond to the gospel with saving faith. Yet the Spirit does even more for us. He testifies of Christ. He is the author of God's Word (2 Peter 1:21). He speaks truth to our hearts, instructing us through Scripture and reminding us what we have learned. He convicts us of sin and draws us to repentance. He strengthens us to put off sin and put on righteousness. He produces fruit in us, such as love, joy, peace, and longsuffering (Gal. 5:22). He helps us stand firm for Christ, giving us the words to say when we need them. He comforts us with the truth of the gospel. He gives us gifts to use to build up the body of Christ. He intercedes and prays for us.

It's no wonder Jesus told His disciples it was a good thing that He leave them: "It is to your advantage that I go away; for if I do not go away, the Helper will not come to you; but if I depart, I will send Him to you" (John 16:7). The Holy Spirit lives within us; He is the very power and presence of God at work in us. Even when we don't feel it, He is at work, molding and shaping us into the image of Christ. He is preparing us for our future glorification, when we will be in the presence of God forever.

Paul tells us in Ephesians that the Holy Spirit is God's seal on us, marking us as His own. As letters in ages past were sealed with the unique wax impression of the one sending it, the Holy Spirit serves as God's promise to us: "In Him you also trusted, after you heard the word of truth, the gospel of your salvation; in whom also, having believed, you were sealed with the Holy Spirit of promise, who is the guarantee of our inheritance until the redemption of the purchased possession, to the praise of His glory" (Eph. 1:13–14). As Ferguson notes, "His presence in our life is itself God's assurance that every spiritual blessing will be ours. More than that, this 'down payment' is a first installment of the final consummation of the blessings we will experience in the resurrection."[9]

When we consider this precious gift, we ought to rejoice. It ought to fill us with awe and wonder. The presence of God living within us? The power of God transforming us? The person of God instructing us? What wonder! Spend time studying God's Word to learn more of the Spirit's work within you. And worship God for this marvelous gift.

This chapter contains great news for fearful hearts. When we fear lesser things, we can look at all God has done for us. From life and breath to the wonders of this created world, from the incarnation to our justification, from the gift of the Spirit to our sure hope of glorification, our God has done amazing

> *If God has given us the greatest gift of all—His Son—how can we think He won't meet us where we are in our fears?*

things. He has given us riches beyond measure. As Paul wrote in Romans, "He who did not spare His own Son, but delivered Him up for us all, how shall He not with Him also freely give us all things?" (8:32). If God has given us the greatest gift

---

9. Sinclair Ferguson, *Let's Study Ephesians* (Edinburgh: Banner of Truth, 2005), 20.

of all—His Son—how can we think He won't meet us where we are in our fears? How can we think He won't provide for our needs? How can we think He won't deliver us or help us or be with us?

Let us consider these gifts God has given us, and may they help us grow in our fear of Him.

Chapter 5

GROWING IN THE FEAR OF THE LORD

Growth in learning anything takes time and practice. This is a lesson I've taught my children. After all, they'd like to ride a bike the first time they try, hit a home run the first time at bat, or get an *A* on the spelling test without first learning the words. But life doesn't work that way. To attain anything, we have to work at it, practicing it over and over. In terms of our topic, the fear of the Lord must become a habit, the rhythm of our soul, one so ingrained in us that it becomes our natural response.

Any Olympian will testify to the hours and hours they've spent training for their sport. Any author will tell you how much time they've spent constructing just one sentence. Any teacher will confirm what it takes to get a student to progress from understanding simple math to algebra—learning, practice, work, growth.

So far we've looked at what the Bible teaches us about our fears and that we are called to replace our lesser fears with a fear of the Lord. We learned what the fear of the Lord is and why we are to fear Him. In this chapter, we will talk about practical ways to grow in our fear of the Lord because fear of the Lord is something that can be learned. The psalmist confirms this: "Come, you children, listen to me; I will teach you the fear of the LORD" (Ps. 34:11).

But I'd like to begin with a caution, something to remember as you move forward. The fear of the Lord is not like a formula you apply to your fearful situations; it's not a magic potion. Nor is it like the responses well-meaning friends might give when they say something like, "You just need more faith, then you'll no longer be afraid." Fearing the Lord doesn't mean you will never again feel any fearful emotions in the face of troubling circumstances. Rather, the fear of the Lord is the posture of your heart in the face of life's fearful situations. It's realizing that even when you stand before something fearful, there is One greater who stands beside you. It is trusting, depending, loving, worshiping, adoring, obeying, and honoring God above all else—even when what you face seems too hard and too frightening. It also means your lesser fears won't rule you and direct your life; instead, you'll hand them over to the One who rules over all.

You may wonder, How do I get to that point? How can I grow in the fear of the Lord? How can I develop this fear so that it becomes a natural response? The first thing to note is that like all areas of the Christian life, growth in the fear of the Lord is a work of God's grace in and through us. While

> *Fearing the Lord doesn't mean you will never again feel any fearful emotions in the face of troubling circumstances. Rather, the fear of the Lord is the posture of your heart in the face of life's fearful situations.*

there is work we are called to do, ultimately it is God who produces the fruit in us. As Peter wrote, "His divine power has given to us all things that pertain to life and godliness, through the knowledge of Him who called us by glory and virtue" (2 Peter 1:3). We are not left on our own to generate this godly fear; God provides all we need to produce and grow in it. What grace! The Lord calls us to a holy fear and then gives us just what we need to live it out. Let's look at a few graces He gives us to aid us in that growth.

The Importance of the Good News

I grew up in the church, and if you were to ask me about the gospel when I was a child, I would have described it as good news for the lost. But I wouldn't have thought it was good news for me. As a child, I misunderstood how far-reaching the good news is; I thought it was just for those who didn't know Christ. They needed to hear the good news of what Jesus had done for them, and once they made a profession of faith, their need for the gospel was over.

As an adult, I've since learned that I too need the gospel. I too need to remember and dwell on the story of what Jesus has done for me. It's not a story I read once and then move on to something else. It's not like reading a compelling story in the newspaper one morning and then tossing it into the recycling bin or reading an informative email and then deleting it. We *never* move beyond our need for the gospel of grace. It's news we need to hear over and over. It's like setting our favorite song on repeat. In his letter to the church at Rome, Paul explained why this news is so important: "I am not ashamed of the gospel of Christ, for it is the power of

God to salvation for everyone who believes, for the Jew first and also for the Greek. For in it the righteousness of God is revealed from faith to faith; as it is written, 'The just shall live by faith'" (Rom. 1:16–17). We live by faith in the gospel, for it is the apex of God's redemption story. It is the truth our hearts need most.

To grow in a holy fear of God, we need to appropriate the truths of the gospel to our lives each day. The gospel story is one we need to tell ourselves over and over. As Flavel wrote, "The first rule for relieving slavish fear is to consider seriously and study thoroughly the covenant of grace in which all believers stand."[1] Theologians say we should preach the gospel to ourselves. We do this by retelling the story of redemption to our hearts. We look to the incarnation, as God the Son left the glories of heaven to wrap Himself in human flesh. We remember that Jesus was born of a woman into this fallen world, where He experienced all the sorrows, heart-aches, troubles, poverties, temptations, and cares of this life that we know all too well—yet He never sinned. He lived a perfect life in our place, fulfilling the law for us. We look to the cross, where He bore the wrath of God in our place and died the death we deserve. We also look beyond the cross to the empty tomb. Because He was righteous, the grave could not hold Him. After three days, He rose in triumph, conquering sin and death once and for all.

We apply these truths to our lives when we are convicted of sin and need to confess and repent of it. We apply these truths when we feel shame over our sin and want to hide

---

1. Flavel, *Triumphing Over Sinful Fear*, 63.

from God. We apply these truths when we forget who we are in Christ and need to remember God's great love for us. We apply these truths when we need to see God as bigger than the circumstances of our lives.

The more we dwell on the good news, the more we see the depth and breadth of God's grace for us in Christ. We can't help but respond in awe, wonder, gratitude, and love. And we can say with the psalmist,

> The LORD is my strength and my shield;
> My heart trusted in Him, and I am helped;
> Therefore my heart greatly rejoices,
> And with my song I will praise Him.
> (Ps. 28:7)

Make it a daily habit to ask yourself, What does the gospel have to say about _____? Whatever the circumstance, whatever the occasion, look to the gospel and remind yourself of who Christ is and what He has done. When you pray, apply the gospel to your prayers, praying through the truths of redemption. Listen to music that reminds you of the gospel— a good place to start is Newton's "Amazing Grace."

The good news is the best news, both at the start of our salvation and throughout our life of faith.

Remembering God's Works

I don't know about you, but I have a lousy memory. Just this morning I walked into a room to retrieve something and walked out without doing so. The more I have going on in my life, the more likely I am to forget an appointment or task

I need to complete. I set reminders on my phone, write lists, and put everything on my calendar.

We are a forgetful people. We forget names, birthdays, and passwords. But worse, we forget who God is and what He has done.

One year my husband nearly lost his job. It was a frightening time, not knowing what would happen. Would he lose it or keep it? If he lost his job, would he be able to find other work? Would we be able to pay the bills? I found myself worried and anxious. During those fretful months, I forgot all the ways the Lord had provided for me in my life, the decades of evidence of His faithfulness. The numerous times in the past when I lacked what I needed, and He met that need. Because I forgot, I was filled with fear of lesser things and not a fear of the Lord.

The Israelites were forgetful as well. When Moses came to deliver them from slavery to Pharaoh, they saw amazing signs and wonders. They saw the ten plagues: the river turned to blood, the frogs and cicadas, and utter darkness stretched across the land. They saw the angel of death pass over their homes while the rest of Egypt woke up the next morning to the death of all their firstborn. They witnessed the parting of the Red Sea so they could walk through to safety on the other side. They then

> *We too need to consider the works of the Lord, lest we forget as Israel did and grumble and complain. Lest we turn our hearts from God and think that returning to a life of slavery to our lesser fears would be easier. Lest we turn to false idols in the hopes they will rescue us.*

watched Pharaoh and his army swallowed up whole as the sea folded over them.

But the first time they felt hunger, they responded, "Oh, that we had died by the hand of the LORD in the land of Egypt, when we sat by the pots of meat and when we ate bread to the full! For you have brought us out into this wilderness to kill this whole assembly with hunger" (Ex. 16:3). They forgot God's miraculous wonders and provision and immediately turned their hearts back to Egypt.

This became a pattern for God's people. Whenever they faced difficulty, they grumbled. They defied Moses. They longed to return to slavery. They even constructed a golden calf to worship out of fear that Moses would not return from the mountain to lead them (Exodus 32). Everything became bigger to them than the God who had rescued and redeemed them. They forgot the works of the Lord.

God then instilled into their yearly calendar ways for them to remember Him. From the Sabbath to yearly festivals, celebrations to remembrances, Israel learned the importance of remembering and reflecting on who God is and what He has done. In Psalm 78:4, the psalmist exhorts God's people to remember God's works, incorporating this remembrance into their worship through song:

> We will not hide them from their children,
> Telling to the generation to come the praises of the
>   LORD,
> And His strength and His wonderful works that He
>   has done.

We too need to consider the works of the Lord, lest we forget as Israel did and grumble and complain. Lest we turn our hearts from God and think that returning to a life of slavery to our lesser fears would be easier. Lest we turn to false idols in the hopes they will rescue us.

We can remind ourselves that God is Creator by stepping away from our concrete jungles and exploring His handiwork in creation. When we hear the ocean's roar or stand at the base of a mountain jutting high into the heavens, we can exalt and praise our Creator for His works. We can keep track of our prayer requests and the Lord's answers to those prayers, responding with thanksgiving for His faithfulness to hear us. We can remember that God is Jehovah Jireh, the God who provides for the needs of His people. We can dwell on all the ways He has provided for us in the past and have confidence He will meet our needs in the present. Flavel wrote something similar: "In order to subdue your slavish fear, you must carefully record your experiences of God's care for you and His faithfulness to you in your past danger and distress. You must apply them to your present fears. Recorded experiences are excellent remedies."[2]

All God's works are good. Let us reflect on those works, recording them so we don't fail to remember.

Reading and Studying God's Word

Our God is a personal God. He communicates with us. He teaches us who He is and what He requires of us. The primary way He does so is through the Bible, which has been "given by inspiration of God, and is profitable for doctrine, for reproof,

---

2. Flavel, *Triumphing Over Sinful Fear*, 102.

for correction, for instruction in righteousness" (2 Tim. 3:16). Unlike any other book we might read, God's Word is alive: "The word of God is living and powerful, and sharper than any two-edged sword, piercing even to the division of soul and spirit, and of joints and marrow, and is a discerner of the thoughts and intents of the heart" (Heb. 4:12).

Everything we need to know to live for God in this world is written on its pages. The Bible helps us stay on the narrow path. When we obey His instruction, it keeps us from sin: "How can a young man cleanse his way? By taking heed according to Your word" (Ps. 119:9). It is our treasure and is sweeter than honey (v. 103). It instructs us, directs us, convicts us, encourages us, and strengthens us. God's Word is our life (Deut. 32:47).

Above all, God's Word tells us about *the* Word, Jesus Christ. He is God's word incarnated in human skin. "He is the image of the invisible God," "the brightness of His glory and the express image of His person" (Col. 1:15; Heb. 1:3). All wisdom and knowledge are found in Him (Col. 2:3). Jesus is the Bible's main theme. Every passage speaks of Him. He is the hero of the story, the principal character. If you want to know the fear of the Lord, look to Jesus, the ultimate God-fearer who perfectly feared the Lord in our place (Isa. 11:3).

To grow in the fear of the Lord, God's Word is where we want to direct our focus. Everything we need to know about God and why we are to fear Him is found in its pages. As Ed Welch notes, "The entire Bible is a textbook on the fear of the Lord."[3] Indeed, if we are not in the Word, we cannot expect

---

3. Welch, *When People Are Big and God Is Small*, 103.

to grow in a holy fear of God. The Puritan John Bunyan spent much time in prison for his faith. He wrote an excellent book on fear. In it he noted the importance of being in God's Word: "For as a man drinketh good doctrine into his soul, so he feareth God. If he drinks it in much, he feareth him greatly; if he drinketh it in but little, he feareth him but little; if he drinketh it not in at all, he feareth him not at all."[4]

As we read and study, we can ask ourselves, What does this teach me about God? We can look for more examples of His attributes and characteristics. We can take note of the numerous names used to describe Him. We can look for evidences of how people respond when they encounter Him. We can learn what it looks like to live in a holy fear of Him. And we can read more of what He has done for us in Christ.

> *If you want to know the fear of the Lord, look to Jesus, the ultimate God-fearer who perfectly feared the Lord in our place (Isa. 11:3).*

Prayer and Communion with the Lord

In John 15, Jesus used the metaphor of a vine and branches to explain how we are to abide in Him:

> Abide in Me, and I in you. As the branch cannot bear fruit of itself, unless it abides in the vine, neither can you, unless you abide in Me.

---

4. John Bunyan, *A Treatise on the Fear of God*, ed. George Offor (London: N. Ponder, 1679), 60, https://www.monergism.com/thethreshold/sdg/bunyan/A _Treatise_on_the_Fear_of_God_-_John_Bunyan.pdf.

I am the vine, you are the branches. He who abides in Me, and I in him, bears much fruit; for without Me you can do nothing. If anyone does not abide in Me, he is cast out as a branch and is withered; and they gather them and throw them into the fire, and they are burned. If you abide in Me, and My words abide in you, you will ask what you desire, and it shall be done for you. By this My Father is glorified, that you bear much fruit; so you will be My disciples. (vv. 4–8)

Though I do not have a green thumb, I understand how a branch receives life from a vine. I look outside my window and see flowering plants, trees, and bushes. I know the essential factors that help them grow and thrive. I understand that a branch cannot grow unattached to the source of its life, nor can it bear fruit on its own. As a result, this passage helps me grasp how I am united to Christ, that He is the source of my life and strength. He feeds me spiritually. He nourishes my soul. He provides what I need. I can do nothing apart from Him. To grow and thrive in my faith, I need to abide in Him.

Prayer is essential to abiding. It is a privilege given to the children of the Father, one purchased for us by our elder brother, Jesus Christ. When we pray we respond to what we've learned in God's Word. God uses our prayers to carry out His will in our lives and in the lives of others. Prayer is also how we live out our unity with Christ. As we pray to Him, we receive from Him all the benefits of our union. In pouring out our hearts to Him, we depend on Him more and ourselves less. We find our hearts reshaped to want what God wants more than what we want. We grow more and more to want His glory and fame spread throughout the world and not our own. Because His words abide in us, we can't help but long for His will to be done in our life. Indeed, prayer not only feeds and nourishes us but transforms us.

John Bunyan exhorts us to pray and ask the Lord to increase our fear of Him:

> Wouldest thou grow in this grace of fear? then be much in prayer to God for abundance of the increase thereof.... Pray therefore that God will unite thy heart to fear his name; this is the way to grow in the grace of fear...for it is the praying soul, the man that is mighty in praying, that has a heart for the fear of God to grow in. Take heed, therefore, of a prayerless heart, if you would grow in this grace of the fear of God. Prayer is as the pitcher that fetcheth water from the brook, therewith to water the herbs; break the pitcher, and it will fetch no water, and for want of water the garden withers.[5]

We can pray at set times as Daniel did. We can pray with a structured prayer as Jesus taught in Matthew 6. We can pray prayers of thanksgiving as the psalmists did or prayers of confession as God's people did in Nehemiah 9. We can pray prayers of lament as our Lord did in the garden of Gethsemane.

We can also pray brief prayers scattered throughout our day. Such prayers come in the heat of the moment, when we encounter fears in our day, when we need God's wisdom to make a difficult decision, when we hear news of a loved one in need of healing. Quick prayers can be prayed anywhere and anytime. We can pray while driving (with our eyes open!), while pushing a grocery cart, while talking on the phone.

---

5. Bunyan, *Treatise on the Fear of God*, 121.

These prayers are part of one long, ongoing conversation with our Lord.

We grow in our fear of the Lord as we commune with the Lord in prayer. As we see Him work through our prayers—transforming our life and our soul and the lives of others through those prayers—we are amazed at His power and grace. We realize afresh how dependent we are on Him. We are humbled that He would work through such weak vessels. And we respond with increased wonder and awe.

Pray and ask the Lord to help you grow in the fear of Him.

Worship the Lord
We've seen that those who encounter God fall before Him in worship. This is the appropriate response from a God-fearer. After all, we were created to worship our Maker. We were made to bring Him glory, as the Lord says in Isaiah 43:7:

> Everyone who is called by My name,
> Whom I have created for My glory;
> I have formed him, yes, I have made him.

We worship God in our daily lives when we live for His glory and not our own. We worship God by giving Him the honor and reverence due Him. As the psalmist wrote, "Give unto the LORD the glory due to His name; worship the LORD in the beauty of holiness" (Ps. 29:2). He alone is God. He alone is our maker. He alone is ruler of all things. Worship is ascribing to God what He deserves: "Oh, worship the LORD in the beauty of holiness! Tremble before Him, all the earth" (Ps. 96:9).

Worship is honoring and exalting our great God. It is thanking and praising Him for who He is and what He has done. We worship Him when we praise Him in our hearts, naming His specific traits and characteristics. We worship when we thank Him for His steadfast goodness to us. We worship Him when we read His Word and pause and marvel at some new truth we've learned about Him. In fact, worship encompasses all that we've mentioned so far in this chapter. It includes prayer and study, remembering God's works, and dwelling on the gospel. We utilize each of those means to bow down in reverence before our wondrous God and honor Him.

> Give unto the
> LORD the glory
> due to His name;
> Worship the LORD
> in the beauty
> of holiness.
> (Psalm 29:2)

God has also called each of His children into organized worship, to the gathering of the saints on the Lord's Day. Jesus promised that wherever two or more are gathered in His name, He is present among them (Matt. 18:20). The book of Acts describes the early church meeting regularly to pray, hear the word preached, and break bread (Acts 2:42). The author of the book of Hebrews exhorts us not to forsake corporate worship (10:25).

Worship with the body of Christ is a unique opportunity for us to live out our fear of the Lord. As we hear the word preached, we are reminded once again of who God is and what He has done. The preacher points us to God's greatness and majesty. He exhorts us to love and obey God in response to all He has done for us in Christ. He talks about sin, the gospel of grace, and the way of repentance. During worship we sing and exalt the great name of our Savior. We feast on the bread and the wine in remembrance of Christ's sacrifice for our sin. All this is worship. All this gives God the glory and honor He is due.

John 4:24 teaches us that our worship involves two things: "God is Spirit, and those who worship Him must worship in spirit and truth." We worship Him in spirit when we worship with our whole heart. We worship Him with sincerity and earnestness. We worship Him out of a contrite and humble heart. Like the one leper who returned to Jesus to thank Him, we worship God from a genuine and affectionate heart that knows the depths of our depravity and the even deeper riches of God's grace.

We worship God in truth when we worship Him the way He has instructed us to do so in His Word. We use His Word to guide us in developing our order of worship. We don't worship Him in a way that exalts us but in a way that exalts Him. We don't design our worship to please the worshipers but to please the One being worshiped. In doing so, we honor God and leave our worship spiritually fed and refreshed and ready to glorify the Lord with our lives.

Grow in your fear of the Lord by encountering Him in worship.

Evaluate Your Heart

When Paul wrote about the Christian life of faith, he used the image of "putting off" and "putting on." Because of who we are in Christ, we are to put off our sinful way of life and put on Christ's righteousness. Like taking off a coat and putting on a different one, we are to put off our former selves, the way we used to live our life, "that you put off, concerning your former conduct, the old man which grows corrupt according to the deceitful lusts, and be renewed in the spirit of your mind" (Eph. 4:22–23). In doing so, we are to put to death sins such as covetousness, anger, malice, and more (Col. 3:5, 8).

Because we are new creations, we are to put on the new man. We are to put on Christian character traits such as kindness, humility, and love (Col. 3:12–14). In our new selves, we are to let the peace of God rule our hearts and to be thankful (v. 15). We are to let the word of Christ dwell in us, so much so that we speak to one another out of that word, responding in praise and song to the Lord (v. 16). And all we do, we do unto the name of Christ (v. 17).

Much of what I've talked about in this chapter has been related to putting on. Now I want to focus on some things we need to put off in order to grow in our fear of the Lord.

Put Off Idolatry

I noted in chapter 1 that our lesser fears center on our loves and longings. Whatever we love more than God is an idol in our heart that we worship. An idol can be anything, including good gifts God gives us. We can worship family, success, affirmation, control, comfort, and more. If we love something and that something is threatened in some way, we may respond with fear. For example, if we've long dreamed of having a specific job, of attaining a certain degree of success professionally, and the dream job is taken away from us, how we respond reveals whether it is an idol in our heart. Flavel wrote, "It is the strength of our affections that puts so much strength into our afflictions."[6]

---

6. Flavel, *Triumphing Over Sinful Fear*, 85.

We cling to what we love most. It becomes our identity. It gives us meaning and purpose. It becomes our very life. If we have idols in our heart, there is no room for a fear of the Lord. So we must evaluate our hearts for loves that compete with a love for the Lord. We must remove them and replace them with a greater love for God.

Put Off Self-Righteousness

At the heart of godly fear is humility. A God-fearer knows she is dependent on God for all things. She knows her wayward heart and the depths of her depravity. She understands the gospel of grace and that she comes to God empty-handed. She doesn't trust in her own works or knowledge or anything inherent in her; rather, she rests in the finished work of Christ for her salvation.

To fear the Lord, we have to put off self-righteousness. We can't trust in ourselves. This includes our theology, our works for the kingdom, the church we attend, or how faithful we are to do our devotions each day. We can't look at people who don't know their Bible as well as we do and exalt ourselves in our eyes. We must put off all these things and put on the humility of Christ as described in Philippians 2, where Jesus "made Himself of no reputation, taking the form of a bondservant, and coming in the likeness of men. And being found in appearance as a man, He humbled Himself and became obedient to the point of death, even the death of the cross" (vv. 7–8).

Put Off Worldliness

Last, to grow in the fear of the Lord, put off worldliness. Worldliness is a love of the world, but not in the sense that you love your neighbors and want to see them come to a saving knowledge of Christ. Instead, worldliness is a love for the *things* of this world, for the beliefs, attitudes, behaviors, and temptations it puts on proud display. As John wrote, "Do not love the world or the things in the world. If anyone loves the world, the love of the Father is not in him" (1 John 2:15). It is a love for things that pulls us from love for God. It is a love for those things that exalts sin. When we fear the Lord, we hate all that is evil and contrary to God and His commands: "The fear of the LORD is to hate evil" (Prov. 8:13).

> A God-fearer knows she is dependent on God for all things. She knows her wayward heart and the depths of her depravity. She understands the gospel of grace and that she comes to God empty-handed.

We are to live in the world but not be of the world. Our lives should not be shaped by the world around us, but by God's word, as Paul wrote: "And do not be conformed to this world, but be transformed by the renewing of your mind, that you may prove what is that good and acceptable and perfect will of God" (Rom. 12:2). To fear the Lord, we must love and serve Him alone. So let us fear the Lord by putting to death our love for what is sinful and pursue that which honors God.

There's still more to learn about fearing the Lord. Next, we'll look at the fruit of fearing God. What happens when we fear Him? What changes do we see in our lives?

Chapter 6

THE FRUIT OF
HOLY FEAR

Each winter my neighbor and I stand on equal ground, at least when it comes to how our yards look—leafless, brown, barren. But then spring arrives, and with it, new life. And then our yards stand in stark contrast.

From spring into summer, I witness pops of color rise throughout my neighbor's yard. Buds on tree branches unfurl into new leaves. Flowers bloom in shades of yellow, red, and purple. The grass is full and vibrant green. Everything is alive and thriving.

I, however, don't know how to keep plants alive. My yard looks pathetic and emaciated in comparison. My trees don't bloom, and if they do, only halfheartedly. For some reason, my daffodils wait until weeks after everyone else's before they make an appearance. And I'm pretty certain something is just altogether wrong with my crepe myrtles; they barely bloom at all.

For most plants, flowers are evidence that a plant is alive and thriving. The same is true for fruit-bearing plants, such as apple and orange trees, blueberry bushes, and grape vines. For most of us, when we want fruit, we purchase it at the store. Few of us grow our own, so we don't realize the process it takes to go from seed to flower to the fruit we eat.

Our family lived in south Florida for many years. Florida is well known for its citrus production, particularly oranges, but in the 1800s a small coastal town near where we lived, Jensen Beach, had a thriving pineapple industry. The industry no longer exists, but to this day, they still celebrate with a festival each year.

My in-laws have a few pineapple plants, and each time I visit their Florida home, I like to check on their growth. Pineapples are interesting fruit. Certainly they are plucky on the outside. They can be difficult to cut. But what makes them unique is how they grow. If you cut off the end of a pineapple and plant it in the ground, about two and a half years later, you'll have yourself a pineapple—one pineapple. That's right, pineapple plants produce only one fruit at a time.

Jesus often explained spiritual truths using the natural world around Him, including plants and trees. In the book of Luke, He taught that good trees bear good fruit and bad trees, bad fruit (6:43–45). He also told a parable about a barren fig tree in which the keeper of the vineyard asked the owner to allow him one more year to see if the tree would produce fruit, and then if it did not, he would cut it down (Luke 13:6–9). We know from a previous chapter that Jesus compared Himself to a vine and us to branches, teaching us that unless we abide in Him, we can't bear fruit.

In terms of our topic of holy fear, if we fear the Lord, we will see evidence of that in our life. We will bear fruit out of that fear. It may take time to grow, like a pineapple plant, but it will grow. While our lesser fears will bear bad fruit in our lives, we can expect the fear of the Lord to bear good fruit. We will explore such fruit in this chapter.

The Fruit of Wisdom

The book of Proverbs is categorized as Wisdom Literature. Written primarily from a father to his son, the book shows the way of wisdom in contrast with the way of folly. Wisdom isn't mere head knowledge; it is applying that knowledge to life. It isn't just knowing the right thing to do in a situation; it is following through and doing the right thing. Proverbs exhorts us to seek after wisdom, to pursue it at any cost. It likens wisdom to a woman inviting people to a feast. Some heed her call; others do not. Some know the value of wisdom— better than pure gold. Others choose the way of the fool and suffer the consequences as a result.

Proverbs has a lot to say about the fear of the Lord. It begins in chapter 1 with, "The fear of the LORD is the beginning of knowledge, but fools despise wisdom and instruction" (v. 7). The fear of the Lord and wisdom are intertwined. Wisdom begins with the fear of the Lord; if you fear the Lord, you will grow in wisdom. That's because God is the source of all wisdom:

> The LORD gives wisdom;
> From His mouth come knowledge and understanding;
> He stores up sound wisdom for the upright;
> He is a shield to those who walk uprightly. (2:6–7)

When we fear the Lord with a filial fear, we desire to learn from Him. We want to follow in His ways. We want to please

Him and do what honors Him. Therefore, we seek after His wisdom.

As we grow in wisdom, we will make wise choices. We will follow the narrow path God has laid out for us rather than the way of the foolish. We will seek God's will rather than our own, for the one who fears the Lord will trust in Him alone:

> Trust in the LORD with all your heart,
> And lean not on your own understanding;
> In all your ways acknowledge Him,
> And He shall direct your paths.
> (Prov. 3:5–6)

> *On this side of the cross, Jesus is wisdom in the flesh. If we want to know what wisdom looks like, we look to Jesus. He lived and taught the wisdom of God.*

In the life of Noah, we see a man who feared the Lord, in contrast to the people around him. At the time of Noah, "the wickedness of man was great in the earth" (Gen. 6:5). God decided He would destroy the world He had made and instructed Noah to build an ark to save himself and his family. Noah obeyed: "By faith Noah, being divinely warned of things not yet seen, moved with godly fear, prepared an ark for the saving of his household" (Heb. 11:7). We can imagine how strange he looked building such a large ship. His neighbors likely thought he was crazy and perhaps wondered where he would even sail the ark. Because they did not fear the Lord, they lacked the wisdom to see that judgment was coming. Noah walked in the fear of the Lord and sought His wisdom above that of the world.

On this side of the cross, Jesus is wisdom in the flesh. If we want to know what wisdom looks like, we look to Jesus. He lived and taught the wisdom of God. Yet God's wisdom seems foolish in the world's eyes. Forgiveness of sins through faith in Christ seems ridiculous to those who are perishing. Seeking to glorify God with our lives rather than our own glory seems upside down to the world. As Paul wrote, "For the message of the cross is foolishness to those who are perishing, but to us who are being saved it is the power of God" (1 Cor. 1:18).

Wisdom calls to us, inviting us to a feast. May all God-fearers hear her call.

The Fruit of Obedience

We obey those we fear. We know this all too well with our lesser fears. If we fear what other people think, we will obey that fear, doing whatever we can to earn the approval of others. We will go out of our way to not upset others. We will strive to placate and please. If we fear the future, we will center our lives on controlling what we fear might happen. We may worship that control by seeking solutions to what we fear and trusting in them as our savior. Whatever it is that we fear requires our obedience. That's why we often feel ruled and led by our lesser fears.

But God calls us to obey Him. Before Israel entered the promised land, Moses prepared them by reminding them of God's law and urging them to obey it, "that you may fear the LORD your God, to keep all His statutes and His commandments which I command you, you and your son and your grandson, all the days of your life, and that your days may be prolonged" (Deut. 6:2). God's people would fear the Lord by keeping His commandments, for obeying God is "the concrete expression of the fear of the Lord."[1]

In the book of Exodus, we see an example of women who lived out their fear of the Lord by obeying Him. After Joseph and his family died, the Hebrews grew in number, and the king of Egypt feared that they would one day rise up against him. So the king told the Hebrew midwives, Shiphrah and Puah, to kill all male babies who were born. The Bible tells us they refused to do so because they feared God (Ex. 1:17). Instead, they saved the male babies. They feared God rather than man, and out of that fear they obeyed God, despite the potential for dangerous consequences from violating the king's command.

As we grow in our fear of the Lord, we'll grow in our obedience as well. As we learn about God's holiness and see ourselves in contrast, as we realize the depths of our depravity and the lengths God went to in redeeming us from sin, as we dwell on who He is and what He has done, we'll grow in our fear of Him. We'll grow in our love, honor, trust, awe, and reverence of Him. And as a result, we'll also desire to obey Him. We won't want to disappoint Him or dishonor Him. We'll find ourselves wanting what He wants. We'll grow to hate our sin and to love righteousness. We'll want to live for Him and follow in His ways. We'll want to exalt His name with our very lives.

---

1. Welch, *When People Are Big and God Is Small*, 99–100.

Obedience is a fruit of a holy fear. Pray for the Lord to develop and harvest this fruit in your life.

The Fruit of Trust

When our lesser fears rule us, they pull us away from trusting the Lord. We find ourselves fretting over the "what-ifs" of life. We worry about the future. We fear what others think of us. We don't try something new for fear of failure. When we hear bad news, our heart despairs.

But as we grow in the fear of the Lord, our hearts yield a harvest of trust. We find ourselves looking ahead to the future with expectation and anticipation, wondering what our great God has in store for us. We know that whatever it is, it will be for our good. We hold our own plans loosely, trusting in God's sovereign plan. We don't agonize over decisions, wondering whether the choice we make is in line with God's will, for we know His moral law and desire to do only that which glorifies Him. Rather than waiting for a neon sign or an open door that smacks us in the face, we move forward with faith, knowing God is walking beside us.

When we do hear bad news—an unexpected diagnosis, a job loss, a broken dream—because we fear the Lord, our heart will be "steadfast, trusting in the LORD" (Ps. 112:7). When other people threaten us in some way, when harm seems imminent, our hearts will turn to the Lord and who He is. We will say with the psalmist,

> The LORD is on my side;
> I will not fear.
> What can man do to me?
> (Ps. 118:6)

We see this trust in the life of King Hezekiah, one who "trusted in the LORD God of Israel, so that after him was none like him among all the kings of Judah, nor who were before him" (2 Kings 18:5). In the fourteenth year of his reign, the king of Assyria took Israel's fortified cities. Hezekiah paid the king in the hope he would leave Judah alone. Then the king of Assyria sent a representative, Rabshakeh, to mock the Lord in front of God's people. He taunted and bullied them, saying, "Do not let Hezekiah deceive you, for he shall not be able to deliver you from his hand; nor let Hezekiah make you trust in the LORD" (2 Kings 18:29–30). When Hezekiah heard of this, he tore his robes in grief and called for the prophet Isaiah and asked him to pray on behalf of Judah. Through Isaiah, God told Hezekiah that the king of Assyria would not capture them and that He would sovereignly intercede to bring an end to the king.

> *But as we grow in the fear of the Lord, our hearts yield a harvest of trust. We find ourselves looking ahead to the future with expectation and anticipation, wondering what our great God has in store for us. We know that whatever it is, it will be for our good.*

Hezekiah then received a letter from the Assyrian king, threatening God's people again. Hezekiah brought the letter into the house of God and laid it before Him. He then prayed:

O LORD God of Israel, the One who dwells between the cherubim, You are God, You alone, of all the kingdoms of the earth. You have made heaven and earth. Incline

Your ear, O LORD, and hear; open Your eyes, O LORD, and see; and hear the words of Sennacherib, which he has sent to reproach the living God…. Now therefore, O LORD our God, I pray, save us from his hand, that all the kingdoms of the earth may know that You are the LORD God, You alone. (2 Kings 19:15–16, 19)

This prayer reveals Hezekiah's holy fear. He was threatened by a king who had already attacked the northern tribes and the other nations around him. Doom seemed certain. He feared the end of Jerusalem was near. So he turned to the One who was greater than the king of Assyria. He brought his fears before the Lord, the great I AM, and exalted His great name. He praised the One who created all things, who reigns above all. He asked his mighty God to deliver His people.

This is what trust looks like in our own lives. When we fear God, we will turn to Him in the face of lesser fears. We will remember who He is and what He has done. We will recall His wonders and His works. We will dwell on His greatness. We will seek His help and hope. The psalmist encourages us, "You who fear the LORD, trust in the LORD; He is their help and their shield" (Ps. 115:11). May this be our trust as well.

The Fruit of Humility

The fear of the Lord and pride cannot coexist. We cannot bow in the presence of our great and mighty God if we sit on our own exalted thrones. We cannot respond to God with awe and reverence if we are elevated in our own eyes. Such pride is what brought the downfall of Satan and his demons. Instead, as Paul wrote, "do not be haughty, but fear" (Rom. 11:20).

The more we grow in our fear of the Lord, the more we'll see the fruit of humility. As we focus our hearts on His great grace for us in Christ, we will respond with wonder and gratitude for His kindness toward us. We realize that our sin is an affront to a holy and righteous God, and we are quick to repent of it. We grieve offending God in any way. We know the terrible fear it is to be outside God's grace and don't want to take the gift of His grace for granted. We treasure the salvation Christ purchased for us. As Bunyan wrote, the fear of the Lord "will make you little in your own eyes, keep you humble, put you upon crying to God for protection, and upon lying at his foot for mercy."[2]

Such humility impacts our relationships with others. We won't compare ourselves to our brothers and sisters in Christ, for we know that we all come to Christ the same way, by grace through faith. We are all on equal footing. None of us comes to God because of something good we've done because no one is righteous or does good. Godly fear expels spiritual pride within us. We don't think of ourselves more highly than we ought. It helps us respond to our brothers and sisters with longsuffering and forgiveness. We don't look down on others for their weaknesses or temptations to sin. Instead, we point them to the gospel and the way of grace.

King David was one who feared the Lord. The Bible describes him as a man after God's own heart (Acts 13:22). This doesn't mean he was perfect—far from it. Yet he loved the Lord, and when he did sin, he responded with humility and repentance.

---

2. As quoted in Joel R. Beeke and Paul M. Smalley, *John Bunyan and the Grace of Fearing God* (Phillipsburg, N.J.: P&R, 2016), 93.

In 2 Samuel 12, the prophet Nathan confronted King David for his sin against Bathsheba. David responded, "I have sinned against the LORD" (v. 13). Psalm 51 records David's prayer of confession:

> Have mercy upon me, O God,
> According to Your lovingkindness;
> According to the multitude of Your tender mercies,
> Blot out my transgressions.
> Wash me thoroughly from my iniquity,
> And cleanse me from my sin. (vv. 1–2)

David responded in humility to the only One who could remove his sin from him. He approached God based on His character, His lovingkindness, and His mercy. He asked to be cleansed and made new. This is the prayer of a humble heart, of one who feared the Lord and grieved his sin.

May the Lord grow in us all the fruit of humility.

The Fruit of Holiness

So far we've seen that God is holy other. Anyone who stands in His presence falls before Him in fear. For some people, that fear is slavish because they are not known and loved by God. They are truly terror-filled because of God's righteous wrath. Others fall before Him in a holy fear, a filial fear, because they are beloved of God. They know they are deserving of God's wrath but have been rescued and redeemed by His grace. They love, honor, and revere His holy name.

When Christ died on the cross for our sins, the barrier that separated us from God was torn in two. God no longer resides in the holy of holies. The priest no longer enters once a year to sacrifice for sin. Our debt has been paid, and we can now enter God's presence with confidence. We can come "boldly to the throne of grace, that we may obtain mercy and find grace to help in time of need" (Heb. 4:16).

As we enter God's presence, we cannot help but be changed. Like Moses, who met with God on the mountain and returned with his face radiant, we begin to reflect God's glory and holiness: "But we all, with unveiled face, beholding as in a mirror the glory of the Lord, are being transformed into the same image from glory to glory, just as by the Spirit of the Lord" (2 Cor. 3:18). We begin to bear the fruit of holiness.

> *Therefore, having these promises, beloved, let us cleanse ourselves from all filthiness of the flesh and spirit, perfecting holiness in the fear of God. (2 Cor. 7:1)*

Some experts say that as we age, our tastes change. When I was a child, I hated vegetables such as beets and brussels sprouts. Now I love them. I also have a well-developed palate for all things bitter, such as dark-roasted coffee and chocolate. This is true of our growth in holiness. When we love God and fear Him with a filial fear, we begin to love what He loves. Our goals, desires, longings, and loves are transformed to reflect what God wants for us. Our taste for sin changes, and we grow to hate it. A holy fear motivates us and stirs us up to live for God's glory. It is the fuel that propels us to cast off what is sinful and pursue godliness. Paul wrote to the Corinthian church about the effects of a holy fear: "Therefore, having these promises, beloved, let us cleanse ourselves from all filthiness of the flesh and spirit, perfecting holiness in the fear of God" (2 Cor. 7:1).

This growth in holiness is a process for sure and one that continues throughout our life of faith. When we are new believers, the Spirit may convict us of more noticeable sins, those evident to other people. The more we grow in the grace and knowledge of God and the more we read His Word and learn about what glorifies Him, we'll witness the Spirit go to work on the sins that lie deeper in our heart, perhaps those not readily apparent to others. He will bring those sins to the light so we can repent and turn from them. This is essential to our growth in holiness. As Martin Luther wrote in his Ninety-Five Theses, the Christian life is one of repentance.

If we are like the apostle Paul, the more we understand God's holiness, the more we see how sinful we are. The longer we walk with God, the more we see ourselves in contrast. It's not as though we are sinning more; it's just that God is opening our eyes to see the sheer depths of our sin. He is gracious in this way, not revealing it to us all at once. Over time, we understand why Paul could say at the start of his ministry that he was the least of the apostles (1 Cor. 15:9) and then toward the end of his ministry that he was the worst of all sinners (1 Tim. 1:15).

Paul summarized the fruit of holiness by calling us to put off sin and put on righteousness, as we saw in the last chapter. May this be our daily task. May we all "put on the new man which was created according to God, in true righteousness and holiness" (Eph. 4:24).

In this chapter, we've looked at the fruit of a holy fear. It's helpful to realize that just like with the fruit we eat, it takes time for fruits like wisdom, trust, and holiness to grow in our lives. It's not a process we can rush. But just like the farmer has joy in plucking the first fruit of the harvest, we too can rejoice at the fruit the Lord develops in our hearts.

Chapter 7

IN THE FACE OF
LESSER FEARS

A few years ago, I had the opportunity to visit Israel and tour biblical sites I had read about my entire life. Each site held important meaning for me and provided greater depth in understanding familiar passages in Scripture. One site, En Gedi, held special significance for me.

In Hebrew En Gedi means "spring of the wild goat." En Gedi is a lush oasis, a verdant site in the middle of the Judean wilderness. What makes it so remarkable is its close proximity to the Dead Sea. Everything in the surrounding area is lifeless. Yet in En Gedi, wild goats roam, feeding off the plants that grow there. A steady stream rushes through the middle of the oasis. Surrounding this stream are rocky cliffs spotted with caves. David hid in those caves while on the run from King Saul in the Old Testament.

Saul was the first king of Israel. He became king after the Israelites insisted that they have a king like the nations surrounding them. Yet Saul did not obey God, and his kingship was taken away from him (1 Samuel 15). This did not happen immediately though. God sent the prophet Samuel to anoint a new king, a shepherd boy named David (1 Samuel 16). Though he had been anointed, it was some time before David became Israel's king. First, he became a musician in the king's court, soothing Saul's tormented spirit with the harp and lyre. Then David stood up to and fought against the Philistine giant Goliath and cut off his head. This won him the praise and acclaim of the people. The women sang in the streets about how many men David killed, comparing him to Saul's conquests—and Saul paled in comparison. Saul responded in jealousy, and from that moment on, he tried to kill David.

> *I cried out to You,*
> *O LORD: I said,*
> *"You are my refuge,*
> *My portion in the*
> *land of the living."*
> *(Ps. 142:5)*

Eventually, David had to flee the city because Saul was determined to kill him. He went on the run, hiding out in the wilderness, going from place to place, with Saul in hot pursuit (1 Samuel 19–23). At one point, Saul was distracted from the chase because of a battle with the Philistines. That's when David headed to En Gedi. First Samuel 24:1–2 says, "Now it happened, when Saul had returned from following the Philistines, that it was told him, saying, 'Take note! David is in the Wilderness of En Gedi.' Then Saul took three thousand chosen men from all Israel, and went to seek David and his men on the Rocks of the Wild Goats."

While David hid from Saul in the caves of En Gedi, he penned at least two psalms, possibly 57 and 142. For me, being able to see the place where David wrote words that encouraged me many times in my life was a memorable experience. I couldn't help but tear up as I looked at the caves and remembered the words he wrote:

Be merciful to me, O God, be merciful to me!
For my soul trusts in You;
And in the shadow of Your wings I will make my refuge,
Until these calamities have passed by. (Ps. 57:1)

and

I cried out to You, O LORD:
I said, "You are my refuge,
My portion in the land of the living."
　(Ps. 142:5)

Where the Mind and the Heart Meet

The book of Psalms has always met me right where I am. Whatever is going on in my life, whatever emotions I feel, whatever challenges I face, there is a psalm that mirrors my own heart. The psalmist seems to describe just what I am feeling in vivid metaphors and descriptive prose. As Calvin wrote, "I have been accustomed to call this book, I think not inappropriately, 'An Anatomy of all the Parts of the Soul'; for there is not an emotion of which any one can be conscious that is not here represented as in a mirror. Or rather, the Holy Spirit has here drawn to the life all the griefs, sorrows, fears, doubts, hopes, cares, perplexities, in short, all the distracting emotions with which the minds of men are wont to be agitated."[1]

The book of Psalms is a hymnbook that was used by God's people in worship. Some churches today continue to

---

1. John Calvin, *Commentary on the Book of Psalms*, vol. 1, trans. James Anderson, Christian Classics Ethereal Library, http://www.ccel.org/ccel/calvin/calcom08.vi.html.

sing from the Psalter, while others sing hymns and praise songs each Lord's Day. The individual psalms were written by a variety of people including Moses, David, Asaph, and other worship leaders. These songs express all the human emotions we feel: from despair to joy, from grief to hope, from fear to trust, from loneliness to thanksgiving.

The psalmist voices to God just what he is feeling—the good, the bad, and the ugly. He cries out for help when enemies pursue him. He rejoices over God's deliverance. He voices deep despair over trials and suffering. He praises God with thanksgiving for who He is and what He has done. He expresses feelings of loneliness and abandonment when friends forsake him. And he remembers God's goodness and steadfast love to His people.

The Psalms are a unique portion of Scripture because they are where the mind and the heart meet. Not only do the words of the psalmist reflect the gamut of emotions we all feel but he always points us to the truth of who God is and what He has done. In these songs, the writer speaks to his emotions the truth about God. There is much we can learn from them about our own emotions, particularly fear.[2]

From Fear to Fear
In terms of our topic—the fear of the Lord—the Psalms are one place (though not the only place) where we see the fear of the Lord lived out in the face of lesser fears. The psalmists experienced fear just as we do. Most often we read their

---

2. To learn more about the Psalms and our emotions, read my book *A Heart Set Free: A Journey to Hope through the Psalms of Lament*, Focus for Women (Fearn, Ross-shire, Scotland: Christian Focus, 2016).

expressions of such fears in particular psalms called laments. These psalms are darker than other psalms; the psalmist tells the Lord what he is feeling and cries out for help. Yet the psalmist doesn't just give voice to his emotions and end it there. He goes further; he turns to what he knows about God. He reminds himself of who God is in His character and what He has done for His people. In these psalms, we see the fear of the Lord weaken and disarm lesser fears. These psalms are a place where we can see the fear of the Lord lived out practically in the face of fearful circumstances.

Let's take a look at a psalm of David in which he wrote about his fear. Psalm 57 is one of those psalms written while he was in hiding from Saul. He had been on the run for a while and was separated from his home and family. Saul was ruthless and had already killed those who had helped David (1 Samuel 22). When would it all end?

1. Be merciful to me, O God, be merciful to me!
For my soul trusts in You;
And in the shadow of Your wings I will make my refuge,
Until these calamities have passed by.

2. I will cry out to God Most High,
To God who performs all things for me.

3. He shall send from heaven and save me;
He reproaches the one who would swallow me up. *Selah*
God shall send forth His mercy and His truth.

4. My soul is among lions;
I lie among the sons of men
Who are set on fire,

Whose teeth are spears and arrows,
And their tongue a sharp sword.

5. Be exalted, O God, above the heavens;
Let Your glory be above all the earth.

6. They have prepared a net for my steps;
My soul is bowed down;
They have dug a pit before me;
Into the midst of it they themselves have fallen. *Selah*

7. My heart is steadfast, O God, my heart is steadfast;
I will sing and give praise.

8. Awake, my glory!
Awake, lute and harp!
I will awaken the dawn.

9. I will praise You, O Lord, among the peoples;
I will sing to You among the nations.

10. For Your mercy reaches unto the heavens,
And Your truth unto the clouds.

11. Be exalted, O God, above the heavens;
Let Your glory be above all the earth.

> *In these psalms, we see the fear of the Lord weaken and disarm lesser fears. These psalms are a place where we can see the fear of the Lord lived out practically in the face of fearful circumstances.*

David's Fears

If you were to look up this psalm in your Bible, you'd see that the preface tells us David wrote this when he had fled from Saul into the cave. In verse 4, David describes his enemies as lions and ravenous beasts. While a wild animal would attack with its teeth, David's enemies are coming after him with spears, arrows, and swords. He is in grave danger and in fear for his life.

We would all feel fear if someone was after us, desiring to kill us. While few of us have experienced this kind of situation, we do know what it is to fear harm. Whether we've received a disturbing diagnosis from the doctor or we hear news of violence in our community or we live through a near-tragic accident, we can relate to and understand the depth of fear David experienced while on the run from Saul.

In the midst of his fears, David turned to God in lament and cried out to Him for help. He told the Lord what was happening and how desperate his plight was. In his lament, we see evidence of David's fear of the Lord.

David's Fear of the Lord

As we learned in earlier chapters, the fear of the Lord encompasses our awe, reverence, worship, and love for our holy, righteous, wise, gracious, and good God. In verse 1, David turns to the One who alone can save him from his enemies. He cries out for God's mercy: "Be merciful to me, O God, be merciful to me!" There is nowhere else for David to turn. Refuge and safety are found only in God.

In verse 2, David references who God is in His power because He is "God Most High." He acknowledges God as ruler over all, including the story of David's life. He also speaks of God's glory, and in a tone of worship wrote, "Be exalted, O God, above the heavens; let Your glory be above all the earth" (v. 5).

David also wrote of God's character in verse 3 of this psalm. He has confidence that God will save him and protect him from his enemies. Most importantly, "God shall send forth His mercy and His truth." And again in verse 10 David is reminded of God's mercy and truth: "For Your mercy reaches unto the heavens, and Your truth unto the clouds."

As David cried out to the Lord, focusing on who God is, he asserted, "My heart is steadfast, O God, my heart is steadfast; I will sing and give praise" (v. 7). Though David was in great fear and was hiding from his enemies, he responded with the fear of the Lord. He sang and worshiped God: "Be exalted, O God, above the heavens; let Your glory be above all the earth" (v. 11).

More than likely, his fears didn't dissipate immediately. He may have wrestled with them over and over. But what we see is that those fears did not rule him. In our own lives, we can't expect to never experience fear. We live in a fallen world, and fear is a human response to the darkness of this world. In a world broken by sin, there is much to be afraid of: disease, loss, violent crime, terrorists, and more. Yet we don't have to be ruled by those fears. They don't have to take over our lives, govern our decisions, and dictate our responses. When we do face fearful circumstances, like the psalmist, we can turn our hearts to what is true. We can remind ourselves of who rules and reigns over all things. We can dwell on the character and goodness of God. We can rest in His sovereignty and His power. We can trust what He is doing in our lives. And as the psalmist did, we can respond, even in the midst of our fearful situation, with worship. In the face of fear, we can respond with the fear of the Lord.

Whom Shall I Fear?

Let's look at another psalm of David, Psalm 27. We don't know the historical circumstances for this psalm. We don't know where David was or what was happening to him when he wrote it, yet it does tell us he was being pursued by his enemies. The first half of this psalm voices confidence in the Lord no matter what fearful circumstances may come his way (vv. 1–6). The second half is written like a traditional lament, in which the psalmist seeks God's help and rescue (vv. 7–12).

> *The beauty of who God is overwhelms his fears and he responds in praise, despite his fearful circumstances. It's a beautiful description of a heart that fears the Lord.*

1. The LORD is my light and my salvation;
   Whom shall I fear?
   The LORD is the strength of my life;
   Of whom shall I be afraid?

2. When the wicked came against me
   To eat up my flesh,
   My enemies and foes,
   They stumbled and fell.

3. Though an army may
    encamp against me,
My heart shall not fear;
Though war may rise against me,
In this I will be confident.

4. One thing I have desired of the LORD,
That will I seek:
That I may dwell in the house of the LORD
All the days of my life,
To behold the beauty of the LORD,
And to inquire in His temple.

5. For in the time of trouble
He shall hide me in His pavilion;
In the secret place of His tabernacle
He shall hide me;
He shall set me high upon a rock.

6. And now my head shall be lifted up above my
    enemies all around me;
Therefore I will offer sacrifices of joy in His tabernacle;
I will sing, yes, I will sing praises to the LORD.

7. Hear, O LORD, when I cry with my voice!
Have mercy also upon me, and answer me.

8. When You said, "Seek My face,"
My heart said to You, "Your face, LORD, I will seek."

9. Do not hide Your face from me;
Do not turn Your servant away in anger;
You have been my help;
Do not leave me nor forsake me,
O God of my salvation.

10. When my father and my mother forsake me,
Then the LORD will take care of me.

11. Teach me Your way, O LORD,
And lead me in a smooth path, because of my enemies.

12. Do not deliver me to the will of my adversaries;
For false witnesses have risen against me,
And such as breathe out violence.

13. I would have lost heart, unless I had believed
That I would see the goodness of the LORD
In the land of the living.

14. Wait on the LORD;
Be of good courage,
And He shall strengthen your heart;
Wait, I say, on the LORD!

As we learned when we looked at Matthew 10:26–31 in an earlier chapter, the Bible teaches us that the fear of the Lord disarms our lesser fears. In verse 1, the psalmist affirms this truth. Compared to God, what power do our lesser fears have? He is our salvation. What can man do to us that God cannot rule over and rescue us from? In verse 3, David writes that even when trouble comes knocking on his door, even when suffering enters his life, he will not fear it. He is confident in who God is.

If you had one thing to ask God for, what would it be? In the context of being afraid, perhaps it would be help and rescue from what you fear. In verse 4, David says there is only one thing he asks: to be in the presence of the Lord. He desires to worship God in His temple, the place of God's presence.

He wants to be with God. And when he is in the shelter of God's presence, David will sing and worship Him, even with his enemies surrounding him (vv. 5–6). The beauty of who God is overwhelms his fears, and he responds in praise, despite his fearful circumstances. It's a beautiful description of a heart that fears the Lord.

Verse 7 transitions to a lament, with David crying out for help. He asks for God to hear him, to deliver him, to help him, and to protect him from his enemies. He refers to who God is: "God of my salvation" (v. 9). He asks for the Lord to instruct him in the way he should go. A lament is the proper response for the fearful heart. A heart that fears the Lord turns to God for help, recognizing that it is God alone who saves. In the midst of our own fears, it is tempting to turn to false and counterfeit hope. It is tempting to look to idols to rescue and save us. But here we see that only God can rescue us. He is our true help and hope.

Like most laments, this one ends with a response of trust and worship. David believes and trusts God will deliver him. Then he encourages others in their fearful journeys: "Wait on the LORD; be of good courage" (v. 14). Waiting on the Lord requires that we trust in and depend on Him. It doesn't mean we don't do anything. It doesn't mean we sit back in passivity. Rather, it's a posture of the heart. For example, perhaps we received an ominous call from the

> *Waiting on the Lord requires that we trust in and depend on Him. It doesn't mean we don't do anything. It doesn't mean we sit back in passivity. Rather, it's a posture of the heart.*

doctor about recent lab work. We return to the doctor for additional testing. While we wait for the results, we follow through on any instructions from the doctor. We also spend time in prayer, asking the Lord for healing. We ask Him to strengthen our faith. We also read the Bible to remember what is true. We preach the gospel to ourselves. We focus on God's character and faithfulness. We ask others to pray for us as well. We continue our labors each day, seeking to glorify God in all that we do. This is the posture of waiting on the Lord. We rest in God's sovereign care, knowing that all things work out for our ultimate good (Rom. 8:28). We trust His perfect plan for our lives. And doing so gives us courage in the face of fear.

Many believers through the ages have found hope in the book of Psalms. Not only do the Psalms express the emotions we all feel but they also show us how those emotions can be reshaped as we turn to God for help. When we dwell on who God is and what He has done, our fear of Him disarms our lesser fears. As you seek to grow in your fear of the Lord, take some time each day to read and meditate on the Psalms.

Chapter 8

GOD'S PROMISES TO THE FEARFUL

Do you have a favorite promise of God? Perhaps it is a much-loved passage you turn to in hard times. Maybe it is a truth you rely on when life is confusing and uncertain. Or maybe you simply remind yourself that God is with you and for you when it feels as though everyone else is not.

The Bible is filled with promises to God's children; they are almost too numerous to count. He promises to forgive our sins (1 John 1:9), provide for our needs (Phil. 4:19), give us eternal life in Christ (John 11:25–26), and be with us forever (Matt. 28:20). There are also many promises for the fearful, including that of Isaiah 41:10:

> Fear not, for I am with you;
> Be not dismayed, for I am your God.
> I will strengthen you,
> Yes, I will help you,
> I will uphold you with My righteous right hand.

This chapter will focus on specific promises God has made to those who fear Him. But before we look at those promises, it's important that we understand why we can hope and trust in God's promises. We need to understand what it means when God makes a promise. Some Christians look at God's promises and say that we must claim them in order for them to be true for us. We must believe them with all our heart and then they will come to pass. Yet God's Word teaches us that His promises are not true because we believe in them; they don't come to pass because our faith is great. God's promises will come to pass simply because God said them.

Our Promise-Keeping God

When God speaks, amazing things happen. In Genesis 1:3, God merely spoke, and light entered the world. When Jesus was on the boat with the disciples and a ferocious storm rose up, He said simply, "Peace, be still!" and there was complete calm (Mark 4:39). When Lazarus was dead in the tomb, Jesus called him out and he returned to life (John 11:43–44). As humans, we can't make anything happen just by the sound of our voice. If we walk into a dark room, we have to turn on the light by clicking on a switch or using our phones to illuminate the darkness. Only God can cause things to happen through the power of just His word, a truth the psalmist expounded:

> Let all the earth fear the LORD;
> Let all the inhabitants of the world stand in awe of Him.
> For He spoke, and it was done;
> He commanded, and it stood fast. (Ps. 33:8–9)

God's word does all that He wills it to; whatever He determines comes to pass. His word never returns void:

> So shall My word be that goes forth from My mouth;
> It shall not return to Me void,
> But it shall accomplish what I please,

And it shall prosper in the thing for which I sent it.
  (Isa. 55:11)

We can make plans for our day and hope that the things we plan come to fruition, but they do so only by the will of God (James 4:15). This is just as true of God's written word. It is alive and powerful. Faith comes through hearing God's word preached (Rom. 10:17). The word sanctifies us (John 17:17). It digs down deep and reveals the motives of our hearts (Heb. 4:12). It is our very life (Deut. 32:47).

As we learned in a previous chapter, Jesus is God's Word in the flesh; He is the Word incarnate (John 1:1, 4). Jesus is the living Word of God. In Him all God's promises are fulfilled. The promise of all promises—"I will be their God, and they shall be My people"—was met in the incarnation and in the perfect life and sacrificial death of Christ for us. His entire life, including His death and resurrection, is a memorial, a kind of ebenezer, of God's steadfast faithfulness to us. Our God is a covenant-keeping God. What He promises to do, He will do.

For those of us who are in Christ, we can know that all God's promises are ours: "For all the promises of God in Him are Yes, and in Him Amen, to the glory of God through us" (2 Cor. 1:20). We don't have to claim them. They already belong to us. All that God promises us in His word are yes in Christ, including His promises to those who fear him.[1]

Let's take a look at some of the amazing promises God has for those who fear Him.

---

1. This section is inspired by a piece I wrote: "Promises Made, Promises Kept," *Place for Truth*, July 11, 2017, Alliance of Confessing Evangelicals, https://www.placefortruth.org/blog/promises-made-promises-kept.

God's Promises to Those Who Fear Him

God Promises Deliverance

Time and time again, God's people faced fearful circumstances, such as hunger and thirst; unknowns; poverty, hardship, and illnesses; and enemies far greater than they. Yet God had promised them, "The covenant that I have made with you, you shall not forget, nor shall you fear other gods. But the LORD your God you shall fear; and He will deliver you from the hand of all your enemies" (2 Kings 17:38–39).

The Bible tells us that the things written in the past are for our instruction (Rom. 15:4). The lives of God's people serve as examples from which we can learn. And there is a lot to learn from Israel! God chose His people out of all the peoples on earth not because there was something special about them, but because He set His love on them (Deut. 7:6–8). He set them apart and made them holy. They were to live different lives from the nations around them. They were to follow His law and walk in His ways. God covenanted to be their God and to dwell among them. They in turn were to obey Him.

When we read the Old Testament, we see what happened. Israel doubted God. They grumbled and complained. They feared the nations around them. Slowly

> The promise of all promises—"I will be their God, and they shall be my people"—was met in the incarnation and the perfect life and sacrificial death of Christ for us. His entire life, including His death and resurrection, is a memorial, a kind of ebenezer, of God's steadfast faithfulness to us.

but surely, they began to go their own way and abandon God's rules and laws. They desired to be like their neighbors. They crafted idols out of gold, wood, and stone to worship and took foreign women as wives. When in trouble, they trusted in false gods and in other nations to deliver them. Throughout the generations, God sent numerous prophets to call them back to Himself, and at times they did return—but never for long.

Our hearts are like those of the Israelites. We too are wayward and wandering. While we desire to obey and please the Lord, we are fickle and often turn from Him. Yet on this side of redemptive history, we have something Israel did not have. We have Someone they looked and waited for: Jesus Christ. He is our deliverer. He delivered us from our greatest enemy, sin; through His death on the cross, He conquered sin and set us free from its bonds. Praise God for His grace in delivering us in spite of our wandering ways!

The Bible teaches us that God is our deliverer, and He promises to deliver those who fear Him:

> No king is saved by the multitude of an army;
> A mighty man is not delivered by great strength.
> A horse is a vain hope for safety;
> Neither shall it deliver any by its great strength.
>
> Behold, the eye of the LORD is on those who fear Him,
> On those who hope in His mercy,
> To deliver their soul from death,
> And to keep them alive in famine. (Ps. 33:16–19)

This psalm points out that we won't find deliverance outside of God. We won't find it in those things we put our hope and trust in such as strategies, goals, lists, blogs, or podcasts. We won't find it in a change of circumstances or a new relationship or a new job. We won't find it in comfort or pleasure. Deliverance is found in God alone.

When you face a troubling situation, when fearful circumstances cut into your life, remember the history of Israel. Their example reminds us that life and hope are not found outside of God. He is our deliverer. May this be true of us:

> Our soul waits for the LORD;
> He is our help and our shield.
> For our heart shall rejoice in Him,
> Because we have trusted in His holy name.
>   (Ps. 33:20–21)

God Promises Satisfaction in Him
God also promises satisfaction to those who fear Him:

> The fear of the LORD leads to life,
> And he who has it will abide in satisfaction;
> He will not be visited with evil.
>   (Prov. 19:23)

This word, *satisfaction*, means abounding and full.[2] Some translations use the word *contentment*. There is a deep and settled contentment in those who fear the Lord.

Contentment is one of those things Christians desire, but it often seems just out of reach. We find ourselves dissatisfied with our work or home or place in life and wish we had greater contentment. It seems like a secret that others have

---

2. *Strong's Concordance*, s.v. "*sabea*," https://biblehub.com/hebrew/7649 .htm.

figured out but aren't sharing. The apostle Paul wrote
about his own content-
ment in Philippians 4: "Not
that I speak in regard to
need, for I have learned in
whatever state I am, to be
content: I know how to be
abased, and I know how to
abound. Everywhere and
in all things I have learned
both to be full and to be
hungry, both to abound
and to suffer need. I can do

> *We won't find deliverance outside of God. We won't find it in those things we put our hope and trust in such as strategies, goals, lists, blogs, or podcasts. We won't find it in a change of circumstances or a new relationship or a new job. We won't find it in comfort or pleasure. Deliverance is found in God alone.*

all things through Christ who strengthens me" (vv. 11–13).

Paul wrote the book of Philippians while he was in jail.
As a prisoner, he relied on the generosity of churches to
support his needs. In those days, prisoners were not fed by
the government. They were not provided clothing or medical care. Family and friends would provide what prisoners
needed. Just before these verses in Philippians 4, Paul mentions that the church in Philippi donated to meet his needs
(v. 10). But ultimately, whether churches helped him or not,
Paul relied and trusted in God to provide for his needs. He
learned to be content with whatever situation God gave him,
whether in plenty or without, because he trusted in Christ as
his strength. He was satisfied in God.

Those who fear the Lord know He is greater than anything they might lack. He owns the cattle on a thousand hills.
He knows our every need. He is a good Father. And we are

known by Him. The God of the universe knows us! He cherishes us. We are His beloved. Therefore, we are always full and satisfied. There is nothing else we need, for we have what our heart needs most: God Himself. That is why the psalmist could say that he would rather be in God's presence than anywhere else:

> For a day in Your courts is better than a thousand.
> I would rather be a doorkeeper in the house of my God
> Than dwell in the tents of wickedness. (Ps. 84:10)

When you find yourself lacking in provision, remember all you have in Christ. When you fear not having enough for tomorrow, remember the One who satisfies your soul. For if God went so far as to give up His own Son to redeem you from sin, how could you think He wouldn't provide all that you need (see Rom. 8:32)? Be filled with the fullness and satisfaction of God.

God Promises Friendship with Him

Friendship is a great treasure. Anyone who has a friend can testify of what it means to have a good friend to turn to for fellowship, understanding, and trust. Friendship is more than just having a few things in common with someone else. It's having someone to rely on in times of trouble. It's having someone who will listen to you; someone who will walk beside you in dark times; someone who will tell you the truth when no one else will. It's having someone you can trust with your secrets, your fears, and your cares.

Psalm 25:14 tells us, "The secret of the LORD is with those who fear Him, and He will show them His covenant." A secret is something you share with close friends, so some Bible translations use the word *friendship* rather than *secret*. We enjoy an intimate relationship with God; He is our friend. God's secret is His covenant, His law, and His commands. Ultimately, His secret is found in the Word made flesh (Col. 2:2–3). God revealed His plan of redemption through Christ: "All things have been delivered to Me by My Father, and no one knows the Son except the Father. Nor does anyone know the Father except the Son, and the one to whom the Son wills to reveal Him" (Matt. 11:27). What a privilege it is to know Christ and be known by Him! Unlike those who have no fear of the Lord, we understand and cherish the secrets of God: "For the perverse person is an abomination to the LORD, but His secret counsel is with the upright" (Prov. 3:32).

Jesus echoed this truth when He said to the disciples, "Greater love has no one than this, than to lay down one's life for his friends. You are My friends if you do whatever I command you. No longer do I call you servants, for a servant does not know what his master is doing; but I have called you friends, for all things that I heard from My Father I have made known to you" (John 15:13–15). A friend is someone who will sacrifice his or her life for another. Jesus did this for us in His sacrifice at the cross. Jesus also said that He passed on all things from His Father, something done not for servants but for friends. We are in His confidence. We know what He treasures and loves. And when we obey Him, we reveal we are indeed His friend.

Friendship with the Lord is a beautiful promise, one that we should relish. I love what Charles Spurgeon once said about friendship with the Lord: "Oh! to be able to say 'Christ is my friend,' is one of the sweetest things in the world."[3] Jesus is that friend who sticks closer than a brother. His love for us is unconditional, born in eternity past. His love is not dependent on anything we've done, for He loved us when we were unlovable. His love is not fickle or temporary. He doesn't make promises and then fail to keep them. He won't turn on us and reject us. Unlike other friendships that come and go, Jesus will never leave us nor forsake us. Jesus not only wants the best for us but He knows what is best for us and ensures that the best happens to us. He works out all the details of our life for our good and His glory. He hears us, comforts us, guides us, knows what we need even before we do, and works in us, transforming us into His own righteous image.

> *Jesus is that friend who sticks closer than a brother. His love for us is unconditional, born in eternity past. His love is not dependent on anything we've done, for He loved us when we were unlovable.*

Jesus is the perfect and best friend of all.

God's Promises to Delight in You

Have you ever wondered how God feels toward you? Psalm 147:10–11 says,

---

3. Charles Haddon Spurgeon, "A Faithful Friend," *New Park Street Pulpit*, vol. 3, March 8, 1857, The Spurgeon Center for Biblical Preaching at Midwestern Seminary, www.spurgeon.org/resource-library/sermons/a-faithful -friend#flipbook/.

> He does not delight in the strength of the horse;
> He takes no pleasure in the legs of a man.
> The LORD takes pleasure in those who fear Him,
> In those who hope in His mercy.

The Lord is not impressed with the strength or power of His creatures. He is not delighted by what humans are capable of; rather, the Lord delights in those who fear Him. He delights in those who trust in Him for hope, rescue, and deliverance. He is pleased when we depend on His mercy and not on ourselves. We love to give good things to those whom we love and delight in, and God does the same for us: "For the LORD takes pleasure in His people; He will beautify the humble with salvation" (Ps. 149:4).

God delights in us because we rightly delight in Him. As the Westminster Confession tells us, our purpose in life is to "glorify God and enjoy Him forever." We are to live our lives for the honor, glory, and praise of the One who made us. We are to find our joy in who He is and what He has done. When we fear the Lord, when we respond to Him in awe, reverence, worship, and love, He is delighted in us. The psalmist wrote of this response:

> Let all those who seek You rejoice and be glad in You;
> And let those who love Your salvation say continually,
> "Let God be magnified!" (Ps. 70:4)

God's pleasure and delight in us are rooted in our union with Christ. As Jesus prayed in John 17:23: "I in them, and You in Me; that they may be perfect in one, and that the world may know that You have sent Me, and have loved them as You have loved Me." We are beloved of God in Christ Jesus. He loves us as much as He loves the Son. What an amazing thing to consider! But it's not because of anything we have done; He doesn't delight in us because of our good works. God delights in us because of Christ. He looks at us and sees the righteous life Christ lived for us. When we sin, Jesus intercedes for us and God accepts His payment on our behalf. We are one with Christ and enjoy the pleasure of God's delight in us. In fact, Scripture tells us God sings over the redeemed:

> The LORD your God in your midst,
> The Mighty One, will save;
> He will rejoice over you with gladness,
> He will quiet you with His love,
> He will rejoice over you with singing.
>   (Zeph. 3:17)

Let us rejoice in the promise of God's delight in us!

God Promises to Be Your Teacher
Another promise God-fearers enjoy is that of God's instruction. He promises to be our teacher: "Who is the man that fears the LORD? Him shall He teach in the way He chooses" (Ps. 25:12). God will lead and guide us on the path of life. He will teach us the way of wisdom. He will direct our ways: "I will instruct you and teach you in the way you should go; I will guide you with My eye" (Ps. 32:8). The Lord will watch over our path and ensure we make it to eternity.

Jesus taught in John 14 that He is the way, the truth, and the life. Through Jesus we come to the Father. He is the path to salvation and eternal life with God. "And we know that the Son of God has come and has given us an understanding, that we may know Him who is true; and we are in Him who is true, in His Son Jesus Christ. This is the true God and eternal life" (1 John 5:20). We know Jesus and the way to life through the word of God. As we read, study, and meditate on it, the way becomes clearer. Indeed, the path is narrow and the terrain difficult at times, but Jesus has paved the way forward. We see the way He walked, and we follow in those steps. We walk with our gaze fixed on Him.

There are times when we forget the Lord's teaching. There are times when the cares of this life distract us. There are times when our fears cloud the way. There are even times when we set the Lord's instruction aside, for we are fickle and easily distracted. John Bunyan reminds us that even when we do wander from God's instruction, He will make certain we find the way back to Him:

> Well, but the Lord whom thou fearest will not leave thee to thy ignorance, nor yet to thine enemies' power or subtlety, but will take it upon himself to be thy teacher and thy guide, and that in the way that thou hast chosen. Hear, then, and behold thy privilege, O thou that fearest the Lord; and whoever wanders, turns aside, and swerveth from the way of salvation, whoever is benighted, and lost in the midst of darkness, thou shalt find the way to the heaven and the glory that thou hast chosen.[4]

God Promises You Good

In an earlier chapter, we looked at the character of God's goodness. He is wholly good and does only what is good. God also promises good to those who fear Him:

---

4. Bunyan, *Treatise on the Fear of God*, 80.

> Oh, taste and see that the LORD is good;
> Blessed is the man who trusts in Him!
> Oh, fear the LORD, you His saints!
> There is no want to those who fear Him.
> The young lions lack and suffer hunger;
> But those who seek the LORD shall not lack any good
>   thing. (Ps. 34:8–10)

In this psalm, David calls us to experience God's goodness, to taste and savor it. He doesn't want us to just swallow whole what God gives us without pausing to appreciate His goodness toward us. David then calls us to trust God, for He will bless His children with all that is good.

> *Delight yourself also in the LORD, and He shall give you the desires of your heart. (Ps. 37:4)*

The question is, What is the good that God gives us? There are some people who read passages such as this and believe that God will bless them with all material things. Indeed, sometimes He does bless His children with material goods—but not always. There are those who read such promises and believe it means that God will cure them of all their illnesses. Indeed, sometimes God does heal our diseases—but not always.

When we read promises like this in Scripture, we must read them in the context of all of Scripture. We know from other passages that God uses things like poverty, sickness, and other forms of suffering for our sanctification and His glory. We know that He does not promise an easy, carefree life for His children. But He does promise a transformed life. He promises to use all the situations and circumstances of our life for our ultimate good. Sometimes it will be for our good that He heals us from sickness; other times it may be for our good that He does not. Sometimes it is for our good that He blesses us with good jobs and financial compensation; other times it is for our good that we go with less so that we would trust in Him to provide for our needs. Whatever God gives us, He will use it to sanctify our hearts, draw us near to Him, show us our need for Christ, and bring Him glory.

Psalm 37:4 reminds us that when our hearts are conformed to the Lord's desires, He gives us what we want most: "Delight yourself also in the LORD, and He shall give you the desires of your heart." May we desire to taste and see the Lord's goodness. May we want what He wants. And may He shower His goodness on us.

As you can see, there are many promises for those who fear the Lord. And what rich and glorious promises! Because whatever God promises comes to pass, we can expect great things from our promise-keeping God.

CONCLUSION:
A LIFE OF HOLY FEAR

We've come to the end of our journey in learning about the holy fear of the Lord—at least in this book. The journey for our hearts is just beginning. Growth in the fear of the Lord is a lifetime journey, one in which we walk each day of our lives. Perhaps that is why so much of the Bible speaks of such fear.

I encourage you to continue reading and studying God's Word, for there you will find the fear of the Lord woven throughout every book and page. You'll find more and more reasons to fear the Lord above all else. You'll see more examples of those who feared the Lord and those who did not. You'll discover more blessings and promises for God-fearers.

Over time, God will grow bigger and greater in your eyes than your lesser fears. While the fears of this world will always exist—until Christ returns—your fear of the great I AM will weaken those lesser fears. Their grip on your heart will loosen. These fears may linger on the sidelines of your life and remind you they are there, but their power will fade in the face of your glorious God. Whenever a lesser fear threatens, turn to the truth of who God is and what He has done.

I want to leave you with a few follow-up suggestions as you continue to grow in the fear of the Lord. These are habits and activities that will help you keep your gaze fixed on God. We are forgetful people and easily distracted. We need daily practices to anchor us. The following practices will help you in your striving to move toward a life of holy fear.

- Read and meditate on the following passages on a regular basis to remind yourself of how great and mighty your God is: Psalm 139; Isaiah 6; Revelation 5.

- Study the meanings of God's various names throughout the Bible, including those of Jesus Christ.

- Study God's character and attributes. Read books on the doctrine of God. Study and learn about the persons of the Trinity.

- Make it a daily habit to think through and appropriate the gospel in your life. Praise the Lord for what He has done for you in Christ. Use passages such as these to preach the gospel to yourself: John 1:12; Romans 4:23–25 and 8:1; 1 Corinthians 15:3–4; 2 Corinthians 5:21; and Ephesians 2:4–5.

- Take time to be outside in God's creation and exalt Him for what you learn of Him through His wondrous handiwork.

- Read the Psalms and make note of how the psalmists voice their fears to the Lord. Write your own lament modeled after the Psalms, sharing both your fears and your trust in your great God. (I discuss how to do this in my previously mentioned book, *A Heart Set Free.*)

- Keep track of your prayers and God's answers to those prayers. Refer to them often to remind yourself of God's faithfulness.

- Memorize a psalm or other passage of Scripture that reminds you God is your refuge and strength in the face of fears, such as Psalm 27 or 46; Isaiah 41:10; or Romans 8:31–39.

- Listen to hymns and praise songs that remind you of who God is and what He has done.

- Don't forsake the gathering of God's people to worship each Lord's Day. Make worship part of the rhythm of your life. Take time to honor, exalt, and praise the Lord for who He is and what He has done.

STUDY GUIDE

How to Use This Study Guide
This study guide can be used by individuals or with groups.
The purpose of the guide is to help you dive deeper into the
content discussed in the corresponding chapters. This guide
includes additional passages to read and discuss. It includes
questions to get you thinking and processing the topic of the
chapter. It also helps you consider ways to apply what you are
learning to your own life as you seek to grow in your fear of
the Lord.

For individuals studying the book: Read the corresponding
chapter first, then go through the study questions. If you need
additional space to write, consider using a journal to record
your answers.

For group leaders using this study guide: Have your group read
the corresponding chapter at home before you meet. You can
use this guide in one of two ways: (1) Have your group members complete the questions at home and discuss during your
meeting time; or (2) save the study guide to use only during
your meeting time. How you choose to use it will depend on

the members of your group, the amount of time you have together, and their margin for homework. Encourage your group to use a journal for additional writing space.

Always begin with the opening discussion question. If time is limited and you can't go through every question, be sure to do the starred questions (*), always ending with personal takeaways from the reading. Leave time at the end for prayer.

If you want to do additional research in preparation, consider looking at some of the books and resources listed in the footnotes. A few key resources are *The Joy of Fearing God* by Jerry Bridges; *A Treatise on the Fear of God* by John Bunyan; *Triumphing Over Sinful Fear* by John Flavel; and *Running Scared: Fear, Worry, and the God of Rest* by Ed Welch. My own book, *A Heart Set Free: A Journey to Hope through the Psalms of Lament* is another resource to use in discussing many of the psalms mentioned in this book.

Chapter 1: A Fear-Filled Life

Opening Discussion:
What kinds of fears have you experienced in your life? How have you responded to them? In what ways have they impacted your life? Your relationship with God?

Read and Discuss:

1. *Read John 9:1–23. What kind of fear did the blind man's parents have?

   Read Genesis 12:10–20. What kind of fear did Abram have?

   Read Judges 6:11–16. What kind of fears did Gideon have?

2. *Discuss the fear of man, the fear of harm, and the fear of the future. What are some other biblical examples of these fears? Which of these fears have you struggled with?

3. *Discuss the source of fear. How can all our fears be traced back to the fall of man?

4. What is the relationship between idolatry and fear?

5. Discuss the relationship between our fears and our loves and desires. What are some ways we might respond when our loves and desires are threatened?

6. *Read Matthew 26:36–44. What is Jesus feeling as He considers the cross to come? How does He respond? What does this tell you about the natural fears we experience in life? What does it mean to you that Jesus faced such intense natural fear on your behalf?

7. *Read Isaiah 41. What is the source of comfort for God's people (see vv. 8–9)? Why were they not to fear (see vv. 10, 13–14)?

8. *What are your takeaways from this chapter?

Pray Together:

Pray together, asking the Lord to help you take notice of the lesser fears in your life and to help you grow in fear of Him.

Chapter 2: Fear the Lord

Opening Discussion:

Before this study, how would you have defined the fear of the Lord? Is it something you often hear taught and discussed? Why or why not?

Read and Discuss:

1. *Discuss the difference between servile fear and filial fear. In what ways has your heart responded to God in servile fear? What are some barriers people might have to developing a filial fear of the Lord?

2. *Our filial fear is grounded in our adoption as sons and daughters of God. Read Ephesians 1:3–14. What does it say about our adoption? When and why did God adopt us?

3. The Westminster Confession, chapter 12, describes this adoption:

> All those that are justified, God vouchsafeth, in and for his only Son Jesus Christ, to make partakers of the grace of adoption: by which they are taken into the number, and enjoy the liberties and privileges of the children of God; have his name put upon them; receive the Spirit of adoption; have access to the throne of grace with boldness; are enabled to cry, Abba, Father; are pitied, protected, provided for, and chastened by him as by a father; yet never cast off, but sealed to the day of redemption, and inherit the promises, as heirs of everlasting salvation.[1]

Make a list of all the benefits of your adoption. Which ones stand out to you, and why? Which ones do you need to grow in your understanding of?

---

1. *An Exposition of the Westminster Confession of Faith*, Center for Reformed Theology and Apologetics, http://reformed.org/documents/shaw /index.html?mainframe=/documents/shaw/shaw_12.html.

4. Read Hebrews 12:5–11. How does it describe God's fatherly love toward us? How does His fatherhood differ from that of our earthly fathers?

5. *Read Isaiah 8 and look for examples of both servile fear and filial fear. Describe the filial fear God calls Isaiah to. Though doom and destruction await Israel, what does Isaiah say he will do in verse 17?

6. *The fear of the Lord is defined as awe, reverence, worship, and love. What does it look like to have awe and wonder regarding our great God? What does it look like to show reverence? How can we show our fear of the Lord in our worship? What might the fear of the Lord look like in our love for Him?

7. Read Revelation 4:8–11. In this chapter, John describes what takes place in the halls of heaven. What song do the living creatures sing? How do they show a holy fear of God?

8. *What are your takeaways from this chapter?

Pray Together:
    Pray together, asking the Lord to help you grow in a filial fear of Him.

Chapter 3: Fear the Lord for Who He Is

Opening Discussion:

Discuss why the meaning of names is important, especially in the Bible. Share what your name means. Do you know why it was chosen?

Read and Discuss:

1. *Why is it important to know God's name? What does the name I AM tell us about Him?

2. Read some other names for God in Scripture. What names for God do you find in each of the following passages?

   Genesis 16:13

   Genesis 22:9–14

   Judges 6:24

Psalm 23:1–3

3. *Read Psalm 9. What does it say about God's name in verse 10? And which name of God is it in reference to? How does the psalmist respond?

4. What does it mean to be holy? What makes a Christian holy? Why is it important that we take notice when God is described as "holy, holy, holy"?

5. Read Leviticus 20:26 and 1 Peter 1:15–16. What do these passages say about God's people and holiness?

6. *Read Psalm 100. What does it tell us about who God is? How are we to respond?

7. *Read John 10:11–18, 25–30. What does this teach us about God's sovereignty? How can God's sovereignty be a comfort to you when you are fearful?

8. *What are your takeaways from this chapter?

Pray Together:

Pray together, applying what you've learned about who God is. Pray to your thrice holy God, exalting His great name.

Chapter 4: Fear the Lord for What He Has Done

Opening Discussion:
Talk about some memorable gifts you've received. What are some gifts in life we take for granted?

Read and Discuss:
1. What are some of your favorite places to visit that God has made? What does His creation tell you about Him?

2. *Read Psalm 135. Talk about the works of God listed here. How does the psalmist respond?

3. *Read John 1:1–16. What is the significance of the incarnation? How is the incarnation a work or gift of God that moves us to fear Him? See also Hebrews 2:10–18. What are the implications given for the Son of God having taken on human flesh and experienced life in this fallen world?

4. *Define *grace*. How is this word often misused in some church circles? In the world? Read Ephesians 2:1–10. What does it tell you about God's grace?

5. Discuss how God's grace is at work in every aspect of our salvation: election, justification, sanctification, glorification. When we take time to consider God's grace, how should we respond?

6. Read through the lyrics to John Newton's hymn "Amazing Grace." (If you don't have a hymnbook, you can find the lyrics here: https://hymnary.org /text/amazing_grace_how_sweet_the_sound.) Discuss the line "'Twas grace that taught my heart to fear, and grace my fears relieved." How does God's grace teach our heart to fear Him?

7. Read Romans 5:12–21. How many times does Paul mention "gift" or "free gift"? What do you learn about the grace of God and your salvation from this passage?

8. *Read John 16:5–15. What do you learn about the Holy Spirit's work in this passage? What is the significance of His work? What are some ways you take the Holy Spirit's work for granted?

9. *What are your takeaways from this chapter?

Pray Together:

Pray together, thanking the Lord for all He has done.
Take turns praising Him for His many gifts of grace.

Chapter 5: Growing in the Fear of the Lord

Opening Discussion:

Talk about the work it takes to achieve a goal or develop a good habit. Share a goal you worked toward. What did it take to reach it? Next, talk about spiritual growth. How do we grow as Christians?

Read and Discuss:

1. *How would you define the gospel? For whom is it good news? Read Colossians 1:3–8. How does Paul describe the gospel?

2. How might reminding yourself of the gospel each day help you grow in the fear of the Lord?

3. *Read Psalm 78. What are some specific works of God that stand out to you? Discuss God's works in your own life. How has He been faithful? How might focusing your heart on God's works help you grow in your fear of Him?

4. *Read a section of Psalm 119. Make a list of the things you learn about God's word. What does the psalmist learn from it? How does it shape his life?

5. Read John 15:1–7. Make a chart of what you learn about the vine and the branches. What happens when we abide in Christ? What happens when we don't?

6. Jerry Bridges wrote, "Our corporate worship services ought to be characterized by awe, reverence, adoration, honor, and love for God.... It means that God and His glory should be the focal point of our services."[2] How have you seen this in churches of which you have been a part? What can you do before worship to prepare your heart so that you can worship the Lord this way? Read Psalms 99 and 138 and discuss what you learn about worshiping God from the psalmist.

7. *Read Colossians 3:1–17. What has happened to us now that we are followers of Christ (vv. 1–4)? What should our life look like as a result? What are some things you need to put off in your life to grow in a holy fear of the Lord? What are some things you need to put on?

---

2. Bridges, *Joy of Fearing God*, 247.

8. *What are your takeaways from this chapter?

Pray Together:

Pray to the Lord together, asking Him to help you grow in your fear of Him. Pray for the Spirit to be at work in you, helping you put off the things that hinder your holy fear and put on those things that help you grow in it.

Chapter 6: The Fruit of Holy Fear

Opening Discussion:
Do you have a green thumb or does everything you plant die a quick death? What are some essentials to growing healthy plants? Have you ever had a fruit tree? What was it like watching the process of its growth? How does this process compare to spiritual growth in our lives?

Read and Discuss:
1. *Read Proverbs 9. How is wisdom described? How does wisdom relate to the fear of the Lord? How is folly described? How does it differ from wisdom?

2. Read 1 Corinthians 1:18–31. What do you learn about the source of wisdom? How does it contrast with foolishness?

3. *How does obedience relate to the fear of the Lord? Read John 8:28–30 and 17:1–5. What relationship does Jesus's obedience have to the fear of the Lord?

4. *Why is it sometimes hard to trust the Lord? How does the fear of the Lord develop greater trust in us?

5. Many of us fear the future. Imagine if God told you all that would take place in the future. This happened to the prophet Habakkuk. The prophet was grieved by Israel's idolatry and sin. He asked the Lord why He hadn't done anything about it. Read God's response in Habakkuk 1:5–11. This was more than Habakkuk expected. God told him He would punish His people through the Chaldeans. He told Habakkuk the future. How did Habakkuk respond? Read chapter 3.

6. How is pride in conflict with the fear of the Lord? Do you know someone who is humble? What have you learned about humility through that person? What are some essentials to humility in the Christian life?

7. *Read an example of humility in Mary, the mother of Jesus, in Luke 1:46–55. How does she reveal humility in her words? How does she speak of God? Herself?

8. *As Christians, we are called to be holy as God is holy. What is the relationship between the fear of the Lord and holiness? How is holiness a process, just like the growth of a plant? In 2 Corinthians 7:1, Paul wrote, "Therefore, having these promises, beloved, let us cleanse ourselves from all filthiness of the flesh and spirit, perfecting holiness in the fear of God." Read 2 Corinthians 6:11–18 to learn what those promises are.

9. *What are your takeaways from this chapter?

Pray Together:

Pray together through the fruits mentioned in this chapter (wisdom, obedience, trust, humility, and holiness), asking the Spirit to develop and harvest them in your life.

Chapter 7: In the Face of Lesser Fears

Opening Discussion:

What are some things we have to wait for in life? What do we often think about the process of waiting? Have you ever had to wait for the Lord to intervene in your life? What was that experience like?

Read and Discuss:

1. *What is the significance of the book of Psalms? What makes it unique, compared to other books in Scripture? Why do you think so many Christians are drawn to this book when they face the trials and struggles of life? In what ways do you see the mind and heart meet in the book of Psalms?

2. Read Psalm 27 together. While you may not have experienced the kind of fear David felt when he was being pursued by Saul, you likely have felt fear of harm. In your own fearful experiences, what truths about God have given you hope and

courage? How does the fear of the Lord give us the longing David had in Psalm 27:4?

3. *Read Psalm 61. This psalm seems to compile many of the truths we've learned so far. How does it reference the fear of the Lord? What are some of God's traits mentioned? What fruits of filial fear do you see?

4. *Read Psalm 34 and the story that inspired it in 1 Samuel 21. What kind of fears did David face? What does the psalm say about those who fear the Lord? How does David show a fear of the Lord in the psalm? What do you learn about God in this passage?

5. We often think of waiting as doing nothing. What kind of work do we see the psalmist do in Psalm 34 as he waits on the Lord to respond to his cries for help? How does this waiting show a fear of the Lord?

6. *What are some things we can do while we wait for God to move in our own life? How can we use that time well?

7. Choose one of the psalms discussed today and write it out together. (Perhaps if you have someone in your group who has the skill of calligraphy, she can teach you.) Post it in a place where you will see it each day.

8. *What are your takeaways from this chapter?

Pray Together:
    Pray through a psalm together.

Chapter 8: God's Promises to the Fearful

Opening Discussion:

What are some promises of God you cling to? Why do you trust in these promises?

Read and Discuss:

1. *Why are the promises we've read in this chapter only for those who fear the Lord?

2. *Read Psalm 115. What does it say about trust and the fear of the Lord? What are some promises for those who fear Him?

3. *Read Psalm 103. What are some characteristics of God mentioned? What name for God is used? What does it tell us God has done? What are some promises for God-fearers in this passage?

4. *Discuss what the prosperity gospel teaches versus the biblical gospel. How does the prosperity gospel view God's promises? How do we view God's promises in light of the gospel?

5. Read and discuss these additional promises to the fearful:

Psalm 34:7

Psalm 111:5

Psalm 112:1–3

Psalm 128

Proverbs 19:23

Proverbs 31:30

6. *Many of the passages we've read promise things like life, deliverance, salvation, goodness, and blessing. How do we see such promises fulfilled in Christ?

7. Which of the promises you've read stand out to you the most? Why?

8. *What are your takeaways from this chapter?

Pray Together:

Pray together, thanking God specifically for the
promises He has given. Pray that you would believe
them not because you have a great faith, but because
of who God is, our promise-keeping God.